Foreword by **Rev. James T. Pierce**

Raising the Levite

Godly Parenting for the Pastor

Tammy Ejimadu

RAISING THE LEVITE
(Godly Parenting for the Pastor)

For all trade orders and bulk purchase
please contact us on: +234 706 542 7615, +234809 044 7764
tamunonye@gmail.com

Printed in Nigeria by

MIND-QUEST
Email: mindquest12@gmail.com
Tel: 0803 551 6978

Table of Contents

Dedication

This book is dedicated to my beloved parents, Apostle Geoffrey Dabibi Numbere (of blessed memory) and Pastor Dr. Nonyem Numbere. They gave up all for the higher calling to serve God in His vineyard as Ministers and missionaries; living a life of sacrifice and an example to the believers.

Appreciation

My thanks go first to God Almighty, who saved me and has given me this privilege to serve Him. I am ever grateful to my parents, Apostle Geoffrey Dabibi Numbere (of blessed memory) and Pastor Dr. Nonyem Numbere for all their love and support to me and to this vision of the House of Levi.

To my darling husband, Evangelist Victor Ejimadu, thank you for your love and support. Most importantly, for going into God's service full time as a young man, showing practically that the office of the Minister is one to be admired. My children: Chibuisi, Princess and Estelle, I love you.

I am grateful to my family, Eld & Pst Humphrey & Grissel Numbere, Wari, Kaydee, Toki, James, Ziteido, Sena, Tomisin, Aunty Hannah, Johnwill, Orinaba, Apainaemi, Tonye, Duabo, Prinye, Victory, Irika, Iche, Nsan, Onyedika, Faith, Christian, Gloria, Ominini, Daopu, my inlaws and the entire GRA family for giving me such wonderful memories, for their love, care and always being there for me and my family. Thank you.

I appreciate my spiritual parents: Pastor James & Diana Pierce (Pepe and Meme), Rev. Mike Oye, Pastor & Pastor Mrs. Isaac

Olori, Pastor Euphemia Porbeni (Mummy Euphy as I fondly call her), Rt. Rev & Mrs. Jonathan Alao and Apostle & Rev. Dr. Mrs. Frank Aikins. Thank you for your love and being an impact in my life.

I want to specially acknowledge Chief Alabo Graham Douglas (of blessed memory) & his wife, Mrs. Muriel Graham Douglas and Apostle Dr. Zilly & Lady Apostle Gladys Aggrey whose love for my mum and the family after the passing of my dad has been special and outstanding. May God bless you.

From the inception of the House of Levi, these ministers have given us unwavering support – Mrs. Mabel Charles-Davies, Pastor & Pastor (Mrs.) Ibim Alabraba, Pastor & Pastor (Mrs.) Blessing Udoh, Pastor & Pastor (Mrs.) Apelle Iyagba, Tch. Diseph Isikima, Evang. Gloria Nwokocha, Evang. Marian Ohuoba, Pastor Chibuike Ejimadu, Evang. Messiah Elelu, Pastor Ebikebuna Tuesday, Past. Dan Adasi, Pastor Clement Akpabio, Past. & Past. Mrs. John Ndeesor, Pastor Precious Enyeribe (of blessed memory) and the Administration of Greater Evangelism World Crusade. God bless you all.

I also want to acknowledge other pastors, Foundation class teachers who have been part of my spiritual growth at one time or the other – Pastor & Evang Reginald Nwokocha, Pastor & Pastor (Mrs.) Ibim Alabraba, Evang & Pastor (Mrs.) Imeh Akpan,

Pastor & Pastor Mrs. Blessing Udoh and Evang Idriss Samura.
My editorial team – Toki Numbere and Nwakaego Akintoye, I
say a big "Thank You".

The House of Levi has been kept alive by some young men and
women who bought into this vision. Johnwill Otobo, Wari
Numbere, Orinaba Otobo, Victory Numbere, Belema Okpaku,
Johnny Nneli, Duabo Numbere, Fabia Batubo, Favour Ohuoba,
Deborah Mary Obakiri, Christian Titus, Toki Numbere, Samson
Gote, Barine, Tontei West, Prince Daniels, Irika Numbere,
Endutimi Smith, Anointed Riches, Makera Ogiasa, Ruby Leelee,
Siminialayi Nengi, Kaydee Numbere, James Numbere, Fortune
Nelson, Victor Nelson, Inima Okpaku, Honor Kanam, Ijeoma
Idriss-Samura. God bless you all. Your labor in God's vineyard is
not in vain.

To every Levite who is part of this body. Without you, there
would be no House of Levi. Thank you.

To every parent (Ministers) who permitted their children to be
part of the House of Levi, God bless you.

Finally, to everyone who has supported in one way or the other,
volunteers, mentors, resource persons, Pastors and Teachers;
may God bless you all.

Foreword

RAISING THE LEVITE (Godly parenting for the Pastor) was birthed from the heart of a godly woman who, from personal observation and multiple conversations with Pastors' Kids (PKs), sees the dysfunctional relationships that often plague the Pastoral Family. Tammy, along with her four godly brothers, was raised in a spiritually healthy, nurturing home. Her parents, the late Apostle Geoffrey D. Numbere and his beloved wife, Pastor Dr. Nonyem Numbere were the founders of Greater Evangelism World Crusade, a spiritually, dynamic Pentecostal organization that reaches the most remote regions of Nigeria as well as countries around the world with the living Gospel of Jesus Christ.

Her project, her goal in printing this book is to bring the Pastoral ministry, which includes the entire family, back into a Biblical perspective. It all begins with the adopting of the House of Levi Principle, that her family faithfully practiced. In short, it means that a Pastor's first ministry is to minister to his own family.

So often, the author witnessed the disconnect between a pastor and his children – even sometimes his wife. She witnessed first hand the frustration, anger, even bitterness of PK's toward their dads. She often asked, "Why are pastor's children so disproportionately resentful of – even God?" Her book dives into the reasons in great detail and then presents answers, cures for the various pastoral challenges that spiritual leadership often face in raising their children. Lack of demonstrating love to your children as opposed to lavishly expressing love to the congregation, no time for family, not being sensitive to the individual personalities of your children, having unreal expectations for your children, dealing redemptively with your children when they fall – all of these and more are issues that the author addresses.

My only wish is that this book was available when I taught my Marriage and Family class at Zion Bible College. It would have been mandatory reading. This book is a must for Pastors raising a family and those individuals in Bible College looking to enter into Ministry.

I highly endorse this book.

Rev. James T. Pierce
Sr. Pastor, Assemblies of God Church, Faith Chapel
Massachusettes, USA

"A Pastor's home is his first parish."

This book though primarily for pastors' children is for both children and parents of pastoral families. Most often, pastors (that is, Ministers) pray for their children to be godly but do not pray for God's enabling grace to be good parents. We generally take things for granted. The author, Tammy Ejimadu is writing from a firsthand experience as a Pastor's kid (PK) both parents being Ministers of God. She is my firstborn and only daughter among four boys. As PKs, she and her siblings learned to make sacrifices for others like we their parents did. She captures those experiences vividly using them to advise PKs as to what the right attitude to their parents should be.

It is a common notion for Pastors to believe and act like their church members are more important than their immediate family. This kind of attitude often results in dysfunctional families. A simple lesson that the author underscores throughout this book is the axiom, "A Pastor's home is his first parish."

The book is a kind appeal to the Minister, "We, your children need your attention. If you love us, show it." It is full of advice and encouragement for the PK even in the face of discouragement, exasperation, or frustration. She maintains that the ace is in both the parents and children trying to maintain a balance between family and congregation.

If there is anywhere that Satan loves most to unleash his arsenal, it is on the Christian family especially the Ministers' family. I recommend this book as a must-read for the Minister, his family and the church congregation, as it will bless their lives by helping them to have spiritually and emotionally balanced families.

Pastor Nonyem E. Numbere
President, Greater Evangelism Women Fellowship International

"..A must read for everyone in ministry, their children, and the church at large..."

The Book "Raising the Levite" is a practical treatise written by one who is a Levite in her own right. It's a work borne out of the burden of her Ministry and passion particularly to those of her constituency who face the demands and complexity of the ministry of their parents. The truths revealed in this book brings to the fore the arduous task and tight ropes which most times Ministers walk and must give very serious attention as well as the necessary balance for a genuine and fulfilling Ministry.

For many Ministers and God's servants, their story replicates this phrase in scripture: *"They made me the keeper of the vineyards; but mine own vineyard have I not kept"* (Song of Solomon 1:6). Unfortunately, this is the sad story of many "powerful" and sometimes hardworking Ministers who labor daily to deal with the fires raging in the lives of their members and community but losing the battle of the one in their Church.

The book is also a helpful tool for the Levites, children of Ministers who are a special heritage, to learn how to find their place in the Ministry of their parents and not become a burden or setback. Knowing that they are not like any other children, but Levites. Also, to be noted is the over expectations and undue demands sometimes placed on Ministers and their family by the church or congregants which contribute to broken families of Ministers, because of their struggle to build an acceptable Ministry and meet the needs of the ones they shepherd. We must come to terms with the truth that the Minister's children needs love and redemption like any other child.

This book is a must read for everyone in ministry, their children, and the Church at large, particularly those who still have the time to make amends so they can make hay while the sun is still shining as they say. It holds nuggets of truth for a healthy family, healthy ministry, and healthy church.
Have an inspirational reading.

Pastor Isaac V. Olori
International Director, Greater Evangelism World Crusade (GEWC)

"...major on the main thing, our children..."
It's for me a huge effort to encourage ministers to major on the main thing, our children, so they are arrows in our hands not in our hearts. The book can be used for a couples' retreat, family devotions and General church Bible study or retreats.

Rt Rev Dr Alao Jonathan A.
Director, Network of Fresh word Churches. Umea, Sweden.

"...This is divine"
I am not sure I have read any material on this subject so non-superficial, transparent and yet, so deep.

This book is not an indictment or critical but it is like an X-ray of the typical ministry household across denominations and ministries.

I certainly wish I had read this book much earlier in my ministry life.
I salute the wisdom and the courage of Pastor Tammy to write this trans-generational book.
This is divine.

Apostle Philemon Frank Aikins
Founder and the Senior Pastor of Rehoboth Christian Centre and the President of Kingdom Covenant Ministry International, Port Harcourt.

Preface

Sometime in January 2005, I had an encounter with God. It was a defining point in my life that reconciled me back to God after a period of dryness going through the routines. My relationship with Him was rekindled and He put in my heart a burning desire to have a forum just for Ministers' children. I shared this vision with my family, and it turned out they too, had the prompting to do something. It was going to be a forum strictly for Ministers' and Elders' children. It was observed that most were wayward, others were tools in the hands of the devil, some came to church as a mere formality and those who were born again were passive in the house of God. Only a handful were truly born again and active in God's vineyard. This was in contrast to the Levites in the Bible whose entire household and lineage were priests unto God.

The idea to have a forum to address the issues and challenges surrounding Ministers' and Elders' children, encourage one another, and change the narrative was birthed. I would like to especially thank my mother, Pastor Dr. Nonyem Numbere who bought into this vision and began to push to make the dream a reality.

However, it was not until January 2011, six (6) years after, that the dream came to life. The House of Levi was established. I thank my beloved father, Apostle Geoffrey Numbere (of blessed memory) who also threw his weight behind this vision. He was not worried that the public might think this a mockery or that this might open up his family to ridicule. No, he understood there was an abnormality within the Ministers' home that needed to be fixed.

Since then, the House of Levi has grown. We have had at least three (3) meetings per year. The inaugural conference was held in January 2013 and has continued annually since then. By the grace of God, the lives of "Levites" (as we call ourselves) have been touched through these programs.

The primary goals of the "House of Levi" are:
1. To build our relationship with God
2. To foster better relationships with our parents
3. To fellowship together to address and find solutions to the issues that are peculiar to the Ministers' homes
4. To go after our mates: fellow Ministers' children who are bound by Satan, in a bid to rescue them
5. To grow to the point where we see God's work as our priestly inheritance and rejoice in working for God.

We believe that God will continue to sustain us and expand this vision to touch more lives and restore families.

As you can imagine, we have had interactions with a lot of Ministers' children during this period, and the experiences have varied from both extremes, but the underlying factors are very much the same. This book is an attempt to put these experiences on paper and bring to light some things Ministers' children would love to tell their parents. It is by no means exhaustive and also not a final authority on raising children. However, I trust it will serve as a guide and I pray that the Lord will expound every chapter and give you the grace to raise godly children.

Also, I refer to the Minister in the masculine tense. This is because most Ministers are male. However, I do not undermine female Ministers or single parents. See yourself despite what your gender or marital status is and I trust you will learn the lessons as well.

The hymn "God give us Christian homes" written by B. B. McKinney should be the heart cry of every Christian, more so every Minister. It is a beautiful sight to see a home given over to the Lord. May God give us Christian Homes indeed.

God, give us Christian homes!
Homes where the Bible is loved and taught,
Homes where the Master's will is sought,

Homes crowned with beauty Your love has wrought;
God, give us Christian homes;
God, give us Christian homes!

God, give us Christian homes!
Homes where the father is true and strong,
Homes that are free from the blight of wrong,
Homes that are joyous with love and song;
God, give us Christian homes;
God, give us Christian homes!

God, give us Christian homes!
Homes where the mother, in caring quest,
Strives to show others Your way is best,
Homes where the Lord is an honored guest;
God, give us Christian homes;
God, give us Christian homes!

God, give us Christian homes!
Homes where the children are led to know
Christ in His beauty who loves them so,
Homes where the altar fires burn and glow;
God, give us Christian homes;
God, give us Christian homes!

*All scriptures are in King James Version except otherwise
stated.

Chapter 1

The Levites

[1]In Christianity, a **Minister** is a person authorized by a church or other religious organization to perform functions such as the teaching of beliefs; leading services such as weddings, baptisms, or funerals; or otherwise providing spiritual guidance to the community.

In Bible times, they were referred to as Levites. The Levites were descendants of the tribe of Levi.

The term "Levites" is generally used to identify the part of the tribe that was set apart for duties and services in the sanctuary. All ministerial duties in the nation of Israel were handled by the Levites. Within the tribe itself, there were two groups:

- The Priests

---

[1] Wikipedia.org

- The Levites

While every priest was a Levite, not every Levite was a priest. However, they all were of the tribe of Levi.

Who were the Levites?

The nation of Israel consisted of twelve tribes, one of which was the tribe of Levi (Genesis 29:39). Levi was the third son of Jacob and Leah. Interestingly, he did not get a blessing from his father, Jacob. Levi together with Simeon his brother had annihilated the city of Shechem in revenge for the rape of their sister, Dinah. At Jacob's death bed, he declared that the descendants of Simon and Levi would be "scattered in Israel".

> *Simeon and Levi are brethren; instruments of cruelty are in their habitations. …Cursed be their anger, for it was fierce; and their wrath, for it was cruel: I will divide them in Jacob, and scatter them in Israel. (Genesis 49:5 – 7)*

This was the curse that trailed that generation. They went from carrying a curse to being declared as the Priesthood! Not just them but their entire generation. At what point then did things begin to change?

First, we see the family of Amran and Jochebed, from the tribe of Levi chosen by God to bring about deliverance to the Israelites.

And there went a man of the house of Levi, and took to wife a daughter of Levi. "And the woman conceived, and bare a son: and when she saw him that he was a goodly child, she hid him three months."(Exodus 2:1 -2)

Exodus 2 – 4 trails the birth of Moses up to his call and we see Aaron his brother pulled into the mission, becoming Moses' mouthpiece. Indeed, God's ways are not man's, He calls and chooses whom He wants.

In Exodus 28, God chose Aaron and his sons to be priests.

And take thou unto thee Aaron thy brother, and his sons with him, from among the children of Israel, that he may minister unto me in the priest's office, even Aaron, Nadab and Abihu, Eleazar and Ithamar, Aaron's sons. (Exodus 28:1)

This was then fulfilled in Leviticus 8

And Moses brought Aaron and his sons, and washed them with water. And he put upon him the coat, and girded him with the girdle, and clothed him with the robe, and put the ephod upon him, and he girded him with the curious girdle of the ephod,and bound it unto him therewith. (Leviticus 8:6,7)

The next time we hear something unique about the Levites is in

Exodus 32. Moses had gone up the mountain to hear from God and get the commandments. Due to the delay in his return, the people became impatient and demanded that Aaron, make a god for them. Moses returned to an ungodly sight and out of anger, destroyed the tablets of stone. He then made a declaration, calling for those who were still on God's side. Guess who stood out? All the sons of Levi!

> *Then Moses stood in the gate of the camp, and said, Who is on the LORD's side? Let him come unto me. And all the sons of Levi gathered themselves together unto him.* (Exodus 32:26)

Finally, we read about Phinehas, the grandson of Aaron who was very zealous for God. The children of Israel had fallen for the immorality and idolatry of the Moabites and Midianites, for which God allowed them to be ravaged by a plague. As the children of Israel wept before the Lord in deep contrition, one of the Israeli men audaciously brought a Midianite girl into the camp! Phinehas was so angry he took a spear and killed the unrepentant pair. This act of his caught God's attention: the plague stopped. God was so pleased, He established an everlasting covenant with Phinehas and his generation:

> *And the Lord spake unto Moses, saying, Phinehas, the son of Eleazar, the son of Aaron the priest, hath turned*

my wrath away from the children of Israel, while he was zealous for my sake among them, that I consumed not the children of Israel in my jealousy. Wherefore say, Behold, I give unto him my covenant of peace: And he shall have it, and his seed after him, even the covenant of an everlasting priesthood; because he was zealous for his God, and made an atonement for the children of Israel. (Numbers 25:10 – 13)

The uniqueness of the Levites

Below is an excerpt from a talk by Pastor Isaac Olori (International Director, Greater Evangelism World Crusade) on the Levities. It highlights the unique things about the Levites.

- **Separated**

One thing that marked the Levites out was that they were separated people, set apart as Ministers – either Ministers of the sanctuary or Ministers in the holy place (Numbers 16:9). They were not to be counted in a census (Numbers 1:47) or own lands (Deuteronomy 18:2). They were also the only people permitted to carry out the duties of the tabernacle such as carry the ark of the covenant, sing, perform sacrifices, etc.

But the Levites after the tribe of their fathers were not numbered among them. For the Lord had spoken unto

Moses, saying, Only thou shalt not number the tribe of Levi, neither take the sum of them among the children of Israel: But thou shalt appoint the Levites over the tabernacle of testimony, and over all the vessels thereof, and over all things that belong to it: they shall bear the tabernacle, and all the vessels thereof; and they shall minister unto it, and shall encamp round about the tabernacle. And when the tabernacle setteth forward, the Levites shall take it down: and when the tabernacle is to be pitched, the Levites shall set it up: and the stranger that cometh nigh shall be put to death. And the children of Israel shall pitch their tents, every man by his own camp, and every man by his own standard, throughout their hosts. But the Levites shall pitch round about the tabernacle of testimony, that there be no wrath upon the congregation of the children of Israel: and the Levites shall keep the charge of the tabernacle of testimony. (Numbers 1:47–54)

- **Zealous and Committed to God**

When Moses returned from the mountain and saw the children of Israel worshiping the golden calf, he was angry and shouted, "Who is on the Lord's side?". Only the sons of Levi out of the twelve tribes stood out and joined Moses. Moses gave them an order to pick up their swords and kill everyone involved in the sinful act of immorality and idolatry. They went ahead and obeyed Moses' instruction. This was what singled them out: they had a zeal for God, and they did not get involved in sin or compromise. Remember the people who they went up against were their brethren, they were fellow Israelites, not some strangers. They were indeed zealous for the Lord even when their own family was involved. Same as Phinehas, who was zealous for the Lord and turned away God's anger, establishing an everlasting covenant with his lineage.

- **Services**

The Levites were involved in virtually everything in the house of God. Below were their duties:

I. They were in charge of the tabernacle. The tabernacle was the mobile church house which was a tent. They were responsible for setting it up and dismantling it whenever God asked them to move (Numbers 1:50-53; 3:6-9; 1 Chronicles 9:27-29).

ii. They bore the ark of the covenant. It was a symbol of God's presence and they were the only people who were allowed to carry it.

iii. Ministered or served before the ark (1 Chronicles 16:4).

iv.   Custodians and administrators of tithes and offerings.

v.   Prepared the showbread in the tabernacle (1 Chronicles 23:28, 29).

vi.   They assisted the priest in preparing the sacrifice (2 Chronicles 29:12 – 26).

vii.   They were teachers of the law. They taught the word of God and the standards of God (Deuteronomy 33:10, 2 Chronicles 17:8, 9).

viii.   They were judges (Deuteronomy 17:5). Today, you would call them councilors. People with cases would come to them because they were people with wisdom and close to God.

ix.   They were scribes of sacred books.

x.   They pronounced the blessings of the Lord upon the people. As the Levites pronounced such blessings, they were speaking the mind of God and God honored every word they spoke because they were special people.

xi.   They were porters of the door of the temple. Today, we call them ushers or protocol officers. They stood to maintain order in God's house.

xii.   They were musicians of the temple. Singing in the choir and playing instruments were reserved for the Levites. They were the people who worshipped God and ministered before the ark.

Chapter 2

The Minister and his family
(The House of Levi)

I t is a rare privilege to be called by God to serve others. The stakes are high from God Himself. One of the criteria to be a Minister as mentioned by Paul to Timothy is that the Minister must manage his family well. [2]Family means a group of persons related by marriage and blood ties and generally living together in a household. A nuclear family or the basic family unit also called the "elementary family" constitutes a husband, wife and children (if any) whether they be biological or adopted. In ancient times, the term extended to everyone in a man's household (including the servants).

The importance of the home front in the life of a Minister or any church officer is such that domestic virtues are among the

---
[2] Nelson's New Illustrated Bible Dictionary

qualifications for such elevated posts in the house of God.

> *He must manage his own household well, keeping*
> *his children under control with all dignity*
> *[keeping them respectful and well-behaved]…*
> (1 Timothy 3:1 – 5 – Amplified Bible)

The stake is also high from the people or the public. Every action, every statement, every behavior of any member of the Minister's family is run through a lens. One cannot blame the public - the man of God who shows them the right way must very well be able to show his own family the right way and lead by example.

In addition, the Minister and his family are already targets of the enemy by virtue of his calling. His duty is to rescue people from the hands of the devil hence, he must expect and anticipate the devil to attack him and his family. *"Strike the Shephard and the sheep will scatter"* is a great strategy the devil uses all the time. But all thanks be to God who already gives us the victory.

The Ministry is also not one with a lot of earthly gains. You might not drive the latest car or have a mansion to your name or have a lot of money in your bank account.

His family, however, pays an even greater sacrifice. They must "share" their Minister-parent with others, sometimes strangers. Show me a successful Minister, and I will show you a spouse and/or child who are standing by him. Show me a Minister with a large heart and I will show you his family with an even larger heart. How else do you explain the sacrifices to share resources, share their space, and very importantly, share their parents with others?

Growing up, it was a common feature at our home to have people who were sick or in need of counselling stay over so my parents could look after them. The house would be readjusted to accommodate the new guests, they would be treated like royalty. A few would come in with demands such as special meals even though they did not need one, and my parents would oblige them as long as they were under our roof.

I remember a situation where one guest insisted he could only drink distilled bottled water. Whilst the household, including my parents drank sterilized water from the tap, our guest would drink bottled water daily and this lasted for over a year that he stayed in our home. It did not come cheap as we were already a large household of 15 – 20 people. They did this without complaining, not even once. As boisterous children, we got upset at some point because we believed he was taking advantage of my parent's benevolence, so we started refilling the empty distilled water bottles. However, he noticed this because the bottles were no longer sealed and would refuse to drink the water. One of my brothers, came up with the smart idea to pretend and apply some pressure to the bottle like we were just opening it for the first time. Safe to say, we saved our parents a lot of money, he never fell ill and did not die either!

The family of the Minister supports him in various ways. All these sacrifices are done out of love, deep-seated love for their parents. One can say they do not have a choice and unfortunately, a lot of Ministers see it as acts of obedience, fear, and submission rather than acts of love. Your home serves as a place of refuge you can return to at the end of the day and find peace. That home must indeed be a loving one. Have you ever paused to think that your family can make the home uncomfortable for you? Indeed, for some Ministers, their family have already taken the destructive path and their home is no longer their safe haven.

The first message, I would like to pass, on behalf of children of Ministers is that we, your children love you! Many parents do not realize that we love our parents so much. In fact, many times, our Minister parent, is our hero. We could follow you blindly just like Isaac followed Abraham to the point of sacrifice. Isaac definitely had questions in his mind, so he asked his father about the lamb. Abraham's response? God would provide. However, at the point Abraham bound him up, laid him on the altar of sacrifice, and even raised his hand to strike, he surely knew he was about to die but he remained radio silent, followed to the end! For sure it is a foreshadow of what Jesus would do for us, but I would like to liken it to the Minister's child. That is how most of us follow our parents. We trust you; we love you and we follow blindly!

It is such a joy to see your father, with whom you live, transcend to that servant of God on the pulpit delivering God's word with such power and authority. It is beautiful to see the respect he commands; how he helps people and proffers solutions to the needs of people. There is this sense of pride and fulfilment we get just watching you go about the Lord's business. I have heard and seen Ministers' children brag so much about their parents because they believe they can fix everything with one prayer, that they have the solution to every problem, and are the most "powerful" Pastors on earth. Sometimes, this love goes all the way to hero worship.

I agree we do not say it or show it enough. It could be due to the fear that has been inbuilt overtime or the fact that saying "I love you" is not a common practice in our culture (Africa). This is why through the House of Levi, we tell fellow Ministers' children to take time to show and tell their parents how much they are loved. On behalf of all the Ministers' children, we say, "WE LOVE YOU".

Chapter 3

Do you really love me?

You love your reputation, not me!

Believe it or not, many Ministers' children feel their parents do not love them as their own. What they love, is their reputation! We do acknowledge that the Minister is under immense pressure to live up to the standard he preaches. He and his family are constantly under a microscope by the congregation he leads and the general public at large.

Due to this, expectations set for Ministers' families are strict and discipline in times of failure is even stiffer. However, Ministers' children can generally tell when they are being lashed out at because a parent wants to protect his reputation. It can be glaring to them when it is just about "What will people say if they hear that Pastor's child did this or that?"

Parents often make comments like "You want to destroy my ministry", "You will not spoil my name" - and when they are silent, we hear it loud and clear with the extreme reaction at the slightest provocation, the proverbial using a sledgehammer to kill a fly.

Are these actions borne out of love, or worry about keeping up the façade and the perfect image being portrayed?

When a Minister's child feels this way, the result is usually either of two extremes – emotional disconnect or outright rebellion. I have heard a lot of Ministers' children who have run riot say, all they want to do is to tarnish that image their parents cherish so much and want to protect. On the other end of the spectrum, they just develop a deep hatred for their parents, they become cold emotionally and have no affection for their parents well into adulthood.

Children need to know that their parents' actions are out of love for them. Even when discipline is required, they must understand fully why they have erred. This discipline must be appropriate and not excessive. It must be done with love and with the child in mind.

You are capable of love, why don't I see it?
Another question Ministers' children ask is "Why is my father capable of a lot of love, but I do not often see it expressed towards me?"

Some common scenarios: a frantic call from a member whose child is in crisis, you watch your dad, run out to the hospital, no matter the time of the day to be by their side; long hours in church, counselling people; special care for the congregation-taking time to find out how they are faring, regular calls to check up on their families, visiting and praying with them; sometimes, he knows all their names and special occasions.

Then you ask yourself, "Why can't he do the same for me? Why can't he treat me the same way?" The moment it comes to his family, he appears bi-polar (an entirely different person), stiff and unapproachable.

One Pastor's child narrated a story of how she watched from a distance, her dad who would not even spare a moment to chat with her, sit with a family especially their daughters, discussing and laughing for hours. That scene was like a sword piercing through her heart, she never forgot it. Hatred built up for that family in particular who seemed to steal her dad away.

What does this result to? Anger and rebellion just like the eldest son in the parable of the Prodigal son. He was angry and would not enter the house; for the first time, we see him upset with his father.

Some Ministers' children have even gotten to the point where they would have nothing to do with the Church because they feel their parents are more interested in the congregation, or that the congregation stole their parents from them.

This is another reason Ministers' children have become emotionally disconnected from their parents, their relationship is non-existent. They are as cold as ice as adults towards them. You begin to wonder why in old age, the Pastor who was so loved by everyone has none of his children by his side? His family is scattered because they have left him to the care of the Church and name, he cherished above them.

You are capable of so much love, show it to your family first and even more. They want to also experience that loving, devoted Pastor your congregation has come to know. Do not assume they already know that you love them; after all, you do your best to meet basic needs. Love is an action word. Show it! Affirm and appreciate your children. Express your love, tell your child, "I am proud of you, child" and "I love you".

I will use this opportunity to talk to children of Ministers, who feel angry and unloved. Let's take a closer look at what the father of the prodigal son said to his returning son: *"And he said unto him, Son, thou art ever with me, and all that I have is thine" (Luke 15:31).*But the first son did not observe or realize this, and therein lies his mistake. The only way he expected appreciation was in form of a party or a celebration. Since it was not done for him, then his father did not love or appreciate him. Many Ministers' children are like this. You have your expectations of how your parents should behave towards you or express their love.

The father in his way, had shown his son how much he loved him, he had handed over everything to this his son - both the inheritance he had given him previously and whatever there was left - everything was his, he held nothing back. He was completely open to this first son.

Some parents do not have many words, but they do show by their actions, in their own way, their love and affection for you. You can never fully know or understand the great sacrifices they make for family, to see you have food to eat, clothes to wear, and above all become successful in life. Some fathers are not there to chat with you because they have to hustle or work extra jobs just to make you comfortable. Some parents might not know how to say, "I love you", but you might be the only child they allow to wash their clothes, enter their bedroom or be aware of their financial status. Some might go personally with you to sort out your school admission or take you to family meetings. Some might even tell you family secrets, assets that no other person knows. These are special ways - in their way they are saying "I love you". Find those precious moments, treasure them, and know you are loved.

Let's turn the table. This father had provided everything for the first son, he lacked nothing. We can tell from the fact that the prodigal son returned just to be a mere servant because even servants were well taken care of. We never hear that this son had celebrated his father neither had he said "Thank you" for your care. Love, they say is reciprocal. As you expect your parents to show love, they also expect the same from you. Look for opportunities to show your parents how much you love and appreciate them. So many people wait until their parents are dead, then they write epistles as tributes, but the question is this, did they ever say those lovely words while they were alive?

Decide today to show your parents you love them. You could buy a little card, write a note, throw a surprise party, hug your mum and say "Mummy, I love you", send a text message, e.t.c. I pray that God will make you obedient children who will not just obey your parents, but honour, respect, and show them love.

The God who stole my father

Some Ministers' children are also upset with God. He is the one who "stole" their parents, after all! When a Minister becomes so engrossed in his service to God that he forgets or neglects his family, his kids sometimes wonder whether the God he is serving is not interested in them as well.

Unfortunately, Ministers, more commonly than not, can be so focused on the church to the detriment of the home. This has caused a lot of hurt to the kids and they, in turn, act out in hurtful ways.

While Church programs hold almost every day of the week, including public holidays, there's often no time for the family to sit, eat or have fun together. While other kids discuss time out with their parents; as Ministers' children, they have nothing to say. Special occasions like birthdays, anniversaries, school presentations, and extra-curricular events are missed, most if not all the time. Little wonder many Ministers' children are repulsed at anything church related. Ever wondered why most Ministers' children are determined never to marry a Minister or be one themselves? They want absolutely nothing to do with the priesthood because of the absentee Minister-parent.

Find that balance, find time for your family even if it will mean you making sacrifices. Delegate responsibilities to create time for your family. Engage in recreational activities with your family. It can be as simple as playing games in your living room to traveling to your country home, taking a stroll with them, and sharing memories of your childhood. There are so many little things you can do to bond with your family. Be deliberate about it and make time for your family.

The People

Leading people has never been an easy task. We have numerous examples in the Bible. We see Aaron, Moses' "right-hand man", respond to the pressure of the people and build a golden calf for them in Moses' absence. Moses himself had to deal with the whims and caprice of the Israelites - they cried for meat, they cried for water, and at other times, for the cucumbers and garlic of Egypt. Even God got tired of them and Moses had to intercede. Finally, they led Moses to anger, and as a result, he did not enter the Promised land.

We know of King Saul, who got jealous and sought to kill David because the people sang songs of praise, comparing him with David (1 Samuel 18:7). There is also King Herod, who imprisoned Peter because the killing of James pleased the people (Acts 12:1).

Nothing has changed today. No one can please everybody, and

the pressure is the same or even more today for Ministers. If one is not careful, you will find yourself swinging like a pendulum just to pacify the people.

This pressure often trickles into the family of the Minister as feedback is constantly received about their kids' behavior, actions, dressing etc., and in a lot of cases, exaggerated. Unfortunately, many times, parents give in to this pressure and react accordingly.

This is not to say feedback is not important, but it must be done appropriately and with good intentions. The Minister-parent must sieve this feedback and know when to watch closely, take action or simply ignore.

Interestingly, sometimes people are upset not because Ministers' children have behaved badly, but because they are perceived to be given opportunities and platforms to excel.

My family by the grace of God is quite talented and so we were given leadership responsibilities right from children's church, to teen fellowship and this continued through to the adult church.

You would find all five (5) children involved in one activity or the other; leading the choir, leading worship, active in the technical room etc. Then the gossip mill began spinning. "Why is it only the Director's children doing everything?". "Oh, he is running a family ministry, his children will lead worship, then lead the choir, his wife will take the Bible reading for the day and then he would preach." They were upset and felt we were given preferential treatment because we were children of the Pastor. However, there were others who saw it as a good challenge, they gave thanks to God for such a wonderful sight, encouraged us, and prayed that their families would toe the same line.

Thank God, my parents closed their ears to these rumors whenever they got to them. In fact, to them it was a thing of pride, to have your whole family given to the service of God. This was the plan of God from the beginning.

Unfortunately, many have fallen victim to this, Ministers have refused to include their children in training, assign them responsibilities and roles in church or even official capacities they are qualified for on their merit, just because they are scared of what people would say.

Do not fall victim to this. Finding the right balance is the key! Do not run a "family ministry" where your children are unduly favored because they are yours or the reverse where they are disadvantaged because they are yours.

Dear Levite (Minister's child), do not be discouraged by people who discourage you. Your service is to God alone!

Chapter 4

I am Human too!

Many times, Ministers are under the illusion that their children are perfect beings. After all, they are seeds from "holy" loins, dedicated at birth, morning devotions held every morning, fasting every week, with the word of God permeating every breathing, living moment. Their social activities are often religious, they know verses of the Bible by heart, they can even pray down a firestorm. Of course, they are perfect angels who can do no wrong.

Reality check - we are all human! Ministers' children do not live in a bubble. They also have feelings, emotions, and are capable of mistakes. Every possible mistake and issue associated with this world, they can experience as well.

The Bible is clear: We are born sinners. *All have sinned and come short of the glory of God* (Romans 3:23). Yes, your children too!

Hophni and Phinehas, though the children of Eli, the high priest, were just as wicked as Cain. Their heritage did not make them immune from earthly desires. It has not changed today.

Your children also feel lonely, rejected, fall in and out of love, and are tempted to have sex, if not with a stronger intensity.

These temptations, surprisingly, often come from within the church, the very place you would think was a safe haven. The church is not a gathering of saints, but a gathering of sinners, saved by grace. Also, some people who attend church are not yet saved.

The Minister's duty to counsel his congregation and lead them in righteous living also extends to his children. You see, those problems that are brought before you daily, are also their problems. Yes, they are! They are human too!

Do not then be surprised, when your daughter says "I have a boyfriend", or your son is caught in one vice or the other, or they tell lies etc. They are human! They make mistakes as well. Sometimes, the pressure is even more because they are in the spotlight and thus a target of the devil.

They might not have fallen into any vice, but remember to take time to counsel your children, to encourage them to live right. Pay attention to the changes happening in and around them and guide them through.

What is expected of you? Love, support and counsel. The same support you provide in counselling and helping your congregation is what is expected from you. Your congregation have expectations from you as their Pastor. Some of them are:

*   **Secrecy:** When a pastor cannot keep confidential information shared by those who come for counselling, they will not return.

*   **Counsel:** Any person who approaches you as a pastor with his or her challenges, expects you will counsel them, direct them on what to do, and pray with them to find solutions to their problems.

*   **Support:** As a pastor, it is part of your routine to check on your congregants, find out how they are doing, ask about their challenges, and support, pray and counsel them as required.

Now, take all these and apply them to your children. Someone said, prepare your children to be the best but prepare yourself as they might fail as well. If that happens, remember we are humans as well.

Chapter 5

Building Relationships

This might look obvious, but the Minister must build a relationship with his family; he must build personal relationships with each of his children. We have discovered that most times, the Minister goes through the routine, devotion, church programs, provides for the family without actually having a personal relationship. For some, their children cannot have a conversation with them, they do not know their friends, what they like or do not like, and the list goes on.

Some have never said "I love you" or hugged their children. Some dismiss it as not being part of their culture. Learn to say affirmative words to your children such as "I love you", "I am proud of you", "You are a star", "You are a performer", "You are awesome" etc..

Be Open and Approachable

Parents need to be approachable. It might sound funny, but a lot of times people outside the home have more access to the Minister. This should not be the case. Your children should be able to share joys, precious moments, fears, and concerns with you. The truth is if they cannot speak freely with you and share their thoughts, they will share it with someone else and for some, this "listening ear" could be a bad influence.

Give them hugs, lots of hugs. There are tremendous benefits from hugging your child such as establishing a connection, making the child feel loved and safe, appreciated, recognized, etc. This is not just for toddlers but should continue even into adulthood. These actions and words express your love. When you say it or show it, they believe it, they feel it, and will love you right back.

Be practical! Share your experiences. A lot of Ministers' children say, "Our parents behave like they are saints who came down from heaven". Dear Minister, you have not always been this servant of God who serves God fervently. No! All of us were once sinners before we found Christ. Everyone has an experience of the sinful man to varying degrees.

What better way to ensure your children do not fall into the same pitfalls you did than by being practical with them? Share your experiences, whether direct or indirect. Let them know you understand, and you are there praying them through it all. It creates a bond between parent and child.

More importantly, it makes them know they can confide in you. Your children would be comfortable telling you anything. Sin thrives in secrecy and a problem shared is half solved. A young girl once told me how she was raped and when she got home her mother smacked her mercilessly for returning late. She preferred to go through the excruciating pain than to tell her mum she had just been raped. She did not trust her mum enough to share such a humiliating experience with her. Others could never tell their parents when they have feelings for the opposite sex or are on the brink of one temptation or the other. The result is that when caught up in sin, they go under the radar, partly because they know the system so well it is easy to evade suspicion. When everything finally implodes, parents are often blindsided by the outrageous sins, their "spiritual" child has committed.

Unfortunately, the issues often could have been exposed early enough and nipped in the bud if only the Minister had taken time to bond with his child.

Sometimes, even when some have opened up to their parents, their reaction was so extreme that their children have locked up, vowing never to confide in their parents anymore. For example, a girl tells her Minister-parent, that she has a crush and the parent is in such shock that he beats her mercilessly, disgracing her publicly. It takes a lot of courage to lay bare your innermost thoughts and even your sins. For that child to take that bold step, care must be taken, not to shut down the channel of communication. You might never get it again.

Share also your experiences with God. Tell them stories of your walk and work with God, the many ways He came through for you, your spiritual encounters etc. In Joshua 4:1 – 7, Joshua told the men to pick up a stone, one for each tribe from where their feet stood in Jordan as memorabilia. Why? So their children will see it, ask questions and they would have the opportunity to share with them the story of God's mighty power. It is a blessing to have you, a godly parent who has experienced God and have testimonies to tell of your exploits for God. Do not hold back, share with your children. It reinforces what you preach, it tells them that God is real and it will challenge them to walk with God.

Provoke not your children to anger

Children obey your parents in the Lord: for this is right.

> *Honour thy father and mother; which is the first commandment with promise; That it may be well with thee, and thou mayest live long on the earth.* (Ephesians 6:1 – 3)

The Bible passage above is a favorite of parents, for obvious reasons. However, it is a common joke among Ministers' children that our parents do not read the very next verse:

> *And, ye fathers, provoke not your children to wrath: but bring them up in the nurture and admonition of the Lord. (Ephesians 6:4 – King James Version)*

> *And now a word to you parents. Don't keep on scolding and nagging your children, making them angry and resentful. Rather, bring them up with the loving discipline the Lord himself approves, with suggestions and godly advice.* (Ephesians 6:4 – The Living Bible)

Verbal abuse is a major means of provoking a child to anger. When harsh words are often said, mistakes rehashed and used to taunt the erring fellow, excessive nagging or discipline applied, it creates deep emotional wounds which last long after the incident has taken place. Even when you have forgotten the incident, it is usually regurgitated by the child. Trust me, Ministers' children have fantastic memories. They do not easily forget how you said what you said, when you said, what you said. Let your words be seasoned with salt and discipline appropriate for the offense and applied with love.

Learn to say words like "I am sorry", "I apologize", "I was wrong" when you are wrong. Many times, it is easy to apologize to a fellow adult when wrong but almost impossible when the person you have wronged is your child. Sometimes when parents do acknowledge they have hurt their children, they refuse to apologize, but would rather prefer to brush the events under the table, and just expect everyone to move on. Even when they do apologize, it is often a half-baked apology which is mostly justifying their actions, complete with supporting scriptures. While the parent easily moves on, it is not so easy for the child, and the event becomes a painful memory, a festering sore. It also erodes trust and tends to affect the child's future conduct.

Dear Minister, learn to apologize - and I mean say the actual words "I am sorry!" and mean it. When you do so, you model how to own up to one's mistakes, humility, and most importantly, it leads to restoration of the broken relationship.

Chapter 6

Clutching Love

Love is a beautiful thing, and the love a parent feels for a child is deep and lasting. A parent's natural instinct is to fiercely support their child's cause. This is why you see parents standing by their child in public, even though privately they would thoroughly scold him/her.

This love however may lead to fear for their child's safety, and a desire to protect him/her from the dangers of the world. Ministers are all too familiar, through numerous counselling cases, of how wicked and evil this world can be, so they subconsciously clutch and 'choke' their child, all in a bid to protect him/her from the world.

Some parents restrict their children from attending a lot of church programs because they are afraid, they might pick up bad habits. Of course, having friends of the opposite sex is forbidden. In fact, some parents have been known to fly off the handle and assume the worst upon sighting their child having a conversation with someone of the opposite sex! Experience has shown it is worse with the girl child.

Many Pastors' children will not understand or see this as love, and this can lead to rebellion. However, they need to understand that parents are clutching because they do not always know how best to express their love, and they are often worried sick about their children and spend sleepless nights fretting over them.

What are the dangers of clutching?
  a. Your child might find it difficult to build real relationships. Due to this extreme protection, your child will not understand how to form cordial relationships with others. Most times, they grow up with a warped personality; the only relationship they ever know is dad, mum, and siblings where this exists. When they become adults, they struggle also to build and/or sustain healthy platonic relationships.
  b. They become gullible and prone to deceit. A girl who has no male friends will easily be swayed by the first boy who

talks to her. She would wear her heart on her sleeve; if unlucky that the first guy who tries to befriend her is out to deceive her, it becomes very easy for her to get caught in his trap.

c. At the first taste of "freedom", he or she will go all out to experience what is considered "missed moments". Ever wondered why as soon as they are no longer under your roof, they seemingly go wild?

d. They go under the radar. Ministers' children are experts at living double lives while depicting a squeaky clean "public image". Many parents have been shocked to hear the sordid experiences of their children, right under their noses.

What then can a parent do?

a. You do not necessarily have to clutch with your love! Allow them to have and bring home friends, so you can observe. I got this nugget from one of my aunts, Dr. Mrs. Akpana, a long time ago. With your parental instincts and the guidance of the Holy Spirit, you can discern those that they need to cut off and counsel them appropriately.

b. Apply the carrot and stick approach! Not every case requires discipline. Even when applying discipline, make sure there is a conversation afterward and the child understands why he or she had to be disciplined. This is critical especially in teen age.

Caution: Discipline does not necessarily mean flogging the child with a stick/cane, in worst case, physical abuse or verbal abuse. There are different methods of discipline that are more effective such as denying a privilege or hobby etc. Today, there are many family coaches who specialize in teaching parents the various ways of training children with the right tools. Get educated.

Chapter 7

Be Responsible
– Take care of your home

It is the parent's responsibility to provide food, shelter, clothing, and other sundry needs for the family. This responsibility does not end until the children reach adulthood and sometimes extends beyond that. This is even more serious for Ministers, as the Bible says any man who does not provide for his home is worse than an infidel (1 Timothy 5:8).

However, from our interactions, a lot of Ministers only do the barest minimum in this regard. They believe that as long as they have provided food and shelter, it is enough. Many times, there are no plans for their tertiary education, and kids are left on their own to plan for their future once they are done with Secondary (High) school.

There have been cases where children have had to decide by themselves if they wanted to go to the University or learn a trade, with no input from the parents. They end up asking around for assistance and sometimes had to train themselves through school. Many of them say, "My parents do not know how I survive in school, they have no idea how I get my fees or what my grades are."

For some, having to fend for themselves has resulted in their engaging in all kinds of vices like sleeping around, stealing, or joining cults, just to make ends meet. Others might not go that far but develop a deep-seated hatred for their parents and the church.

However, the most serious implication I have come to learn is that many who find themselves in such situations, disconnect emotionally from their parents. Do you wonder why they do not care about you as adults? The reason is that they never felt that warmth or care while growing up because you were not involved.

This might not always be the parents' fault. The truth is, every Minister's home goes through different seasons of lack or want, and a lot of faithful Pastors do not have the resources to always give their children the necessities. This even happened in the

Bible to the extent that God had to intervene.

God had given strict instructions for the care of the priests/Levites and their families. They were to subsist on the sacrifices and tithes offered by the children of Israel.

Unfortunately, by the time of Nehemiah, people neglected to obey God's commandments on this issue, and it affected the tribe of Levi directly.

> *And I perceived that the portions of the Levites had not been given them: for the Levites and the singers, that did the work, were fled everyone to his field.* (Nehemiah 13:10)

Most Ministers' families have experienced this. There are times when compulsory fasts are declared just to cover up for the lack or rent is overdue. There is also the common assumption by the congregation that the Pastor has it all, and many are shocked when they discover the level of lack in the Pastor's home. I pray congregations live up to their duty to care for their Pastors. It is a direct service to God.

Something interesting happened in the account in Nehemiah: the priests took matters into their own hands and went out to look for another means of livelihood. While one might argue that they should not have left off God's work, I am particularly proud that they did something about their situation, so they could feed their families. That is critical! Ministers must take responsibility for their families. There are a lot of options available today for learning or career development. Have an affordable plan to ensure they have a bright future, and make sure you stick to it.

If your wards are still in school, ensure you know the details of their academic performance. Some Ministers' children have failed through school and even dropped out without their parents having an inkling. My parents always checked my results while in the University, and thus were able to motivate me to try harder when my grades were dropping. As a result of their efforts, I graduated with a good degree.

However, it is important to live a contented life within your means and teach your children the same principles. The Bible says, *"godliness with contentment, is great gain."* (1 Timothy 6:6). I have seen Ministers who plan their lives based on the income of their members – some even send their children overseas for school, on the premise that their congregation will pay for such exorbitance. Some Pastors' families put so much pressure on the Pastor to live the high life, complete with vacations overseas and expensive clothing, that some have resorted to stealing church money to fund their luxurious lifestyles.

We would do well to learn from Paul; *"I know how to live on almost nothing or with everything. I have learned the secret of living in every situation, whether it is with a full stomach or empty, with plenty or little."*(Philippians 4:12 New Living Translation)

Chapter 8

Extremes

A lot of times, Ministers also focus on some of their children while neglecting the others. We will look at some extremes that exist.

Focus on the girl-child

It has been observed that there is so much focus on the girl child. Heavy restrictions are put in place and every move is scrutinized thoroughly. The boys, however, are assumed to be responsible and thus totally ignored.

Maybe it is because girls bear the brunt of the results of immorality: pregnancy which may lead to dropping out of school and having to raise a child at a very young age. There is also the stigma that follows single mothers. The boy who got her pregnant, after the initial remorse, is often able to go on with his life as though nothing happened.

Most parents, therefore, tend to be overprotective of their daughters with less or no focus on their sons. They are livid if they find her hanging out with boys but would say nothing if their sons keep female company.

The perception that only the female child is subject to temptation is a wrong one.

Interestingly, because boys are left to their devices, they often end up in vices they did not bargain for, and even worse, they go completely unnoticed because of this "trust" already bestowed on them by their parents.

The care and concern to guide the female child through puberty must also be extended to the male child. He needs counselling, guidance, and love just as much as his female counterpart. Do not leave him to his whims due to the erroneous belief, that just because he is male, he knows how to take care of himself and make the right decisions..

Focus on the rebellious child
The other extreme observed is the focus on the "rebellious" child and neglect of the "good" child.

We see this clearly in the parable of the Prodigal Son. The first son had many wonderful qualities. We only hear of him towards the end of the parable and there we are told he just returned from the field.

He was a hard worker, he looked after his father's property and he was not ambitious – he never asked for his inheritance, unlike his brother. Even though their father gave both sons their inheritance, he did not run away but was content to be under his father. Such children are not easy to come by.

We then see an interesting event in this story: the prodigal son returned, and the father threw a party for him. When the elder son returned from the field, he heard the music and enquired what was happening (perhaps it was a strange event happening in the house). He was then told that his younger brother, who had been rebellious, was the reason for the celebration. This upset him and he would not go in, so his father had to come out and talk to him. He then poured out his heart.

> *And he answering said to his father, Lo, these many years do I serve thee, neither transgressed I at any time thy commandment: and yet thou never gavest me a kid, that I might make merry with my friends: But as soon as this thy son was come, which hath devoured thy living*

with harlots, thou hast killed for him the fatted calf.
(Luke 15:29, 30)

Here was an obedient son, who (it seems) had never been commended or celebrated by his father, neither had his obedience been observed or appreciated. Not even a "well done"; "I love you"; "Thank you, my son, for standing by me".

Unfortunately, a lot of parents are like this father. We tend to overlook our obedient child/children and focus on that delinquent or disobedient one. We never tell our children we love them or set time apart just to sit and talk with them. The father's response is typical – "Son, you are always with me, everything I have is yours". Yes, but how do they know if you do not say it? I perceive that the eldest son's problem was not the fatted calf that was killed but rather the show of love from his father. It was something he had never experienced, and many children are in similar shoes. Someone once said –"If you love me, show it".

The neglect sometimes is not just about commendation for being a good child, but also in terms of guidance and counselling. The child who is well behaved typically does not get pep talks, advice or counsel because he is well behaved. Again, a child left alone is open to exploring and your "good child" might end up gaining new unhealthy habits. Once again, dear parents, please give your children a hug regularly, tell them you love them, that you are proud of them. They are precious words that will let your children know you appreciate and love them. Focus on all your children, whether rebellious or well-behaved.

Neglect of the Quiet Child

This is similar to, but not quite the same as the neglect of the "good" child. The child who is quiet and keeps to himself is also often neglected with the excuse that "He is always like that" or "That is his character". Be careful: that quietness might be a result of underlying issues.

Sometimes, such a child might be experiencing depression resulting from a deep feeling of neglect hence the quietness or reclusive nature. The Minister often concludes that his quiet child is levelheaded and good and has no issues or concerns. This results in the child feeling unloved and unimportant, which could culminate in depression and inferiority complex, or in other cases, rebellion. The parent is then shocked when out of the blue, his quiet child is brazenly going against everything he believed and taught.

Dear Minister, do take time out to engage and relate with all your children, make no assumptions, make no excuses, they all need you.

No Discipline

Another extreme is where the Minister believes his child is an angel and can do no wrong. This could be borne from the fact that Christian traditions in the home are constant and like clockwork - devotions by 5 am are sacrosanct, fasting and prayer done every week, etc., the child may also be active in church activities.

It could also stem from an inordinate desire to defend your child, resulting in being at the mercy of your child and spoiling the child.

People may have come forward to inform the Minister about his child's shenanigans, but because he believes his child can do no wrong, it all falls on deaf ears. Even in the face of incontrovertible facts, the parent lives in denial and does not correct or discipline the child. At best, where some "warning" or "caution" is issued, it is more of a slap on the wrist.

We see such a nonchalant attitude from Eli, the priest.

> *For I have told him that I will judge his house for ever for the iniquity which he knoweth; because his sons made themselves vile, and he restrained them not. (1 Samuel 3:13)*

The Message Bible translates it as *"…He knew what was going on, that his sons were desecrating God's name and God's place, and he did nothing to stop them."*

As a result, God disciplined him and his children, and also replaced him with Samuel as a judge.

Adonijah, son of David, was also never disciplined.

> *Now his father, King David, had never disciplined him at any time — not so much as by a single scolding! He was a very handsome man and was Absalom's younger brother.* (1 Kings 1:6 – The Living Bible)

The result was that he tried to dethrone his father while he was still alive.

We reap what we sow. If this is not curbed, one day you will experience the results of not disciplining your child.

Hyper spirituality

A lot of times, a Minister can be so involved in church that it becomes the entirety of his family's experience. They watch only Christian movies and TV, read only Christian books, and perhaps, the only recreational activity they know is prayer and fasting!

You are choking your child and damning him to growing up with a myopic view of life. When he/she is no longer under your roof, would he/she be able to hold a conversation with his peers?

Is he/she aware of the happenings in society?

Such stifling is counterproductive. Expose your children to a broad variety of experiences, such as in sports, politics etc under your guidance. Help them find the right balance, so when they depart from your abode they will not be lost.

Chapter 9

Behind the Scenes

A Minister once preached from John 1:16 *"There was a man sent from God, whose name was John."* He stressed that John was first a man, before he was sent by God. A Minister is usually placed on a pedestal by his congregation. This is because he preaches the word with unction and authority, and the sermon refreshes the congregation. When he prays, testimonies follow. Thus, he is often thought to be an infallible super being who does no wrong.

However, this could not be farther from the truth. A person does not cease to be a mere mortal just because he has been ordained a Minister.

After all is said and done, he still has to go home where there are no lights and cameras. He takes his suit off and becomes a husband and father. His family is the one that sees him for who he is, they see him when he is weak and when he is strong, he is bare before them, with no airs or graces. This is one of the reasons why your family must be intact because it is your place of safety; they are all you really have.

The Hypocrite in Church

Unfortunately, there are cases where the man at home is the opposite of the Pastor in the church. While we understand Ministers of God are also human, sometimes this dysfunction can only be described as "The hypocrite in church". At home, some Ministers show no single trace of the virtues they preach or portray outside.

The gentle, soft-spoken man of God transforms into a ferocious Lion at home, screaming and sometimes physically abusing his wife and children. The children of the otherwise approachable and gentle Pastor have to plan for days to bring up a matter for discussion in a way that would not unleash his wrath; they see how shabbily he treats his spouse at home and even worse, have stumbled on evidence of extramarital escapades, never mind what he preaches. May our lives be an example on and off the pulpit.

Many Pastors' children have said when they look at their fathers on the pulpit, it is difficult to correlate with the same person at home. Some jeer at their father as he preaches, not listening to even one word that he says, all because they know he is a hypocrite. Never think your children are not aware of how you live and how you treat your spouse. They know more than you think they do! Practice what you preach and be an example of the believer in word and in deed, whether in church or at home.

Church Politics

Like every institution, the church is not exempt from conflicts, power tussles, and disagreements. Severally in the Old Testament, Moses had to deal with rebellion from the people, sometimes led by leaders. At a point, even his own family questioned his leadership (Numbers 12:1,2).

Nothing has changed today. The Minister has his share of church trouble, and he often shares concerns, worries, and fears with his family. Thus, they tend to know more than the average person about what is going on.

However, sometimes confidential information is inadvertently shared with family members, from where it is leaked to the whole congregation.

Other times, when the Minister shares his pain and travails with his family, the account could be biased in his favor, as we all do when narrating, and it can sow seeds of discord and hatred in the hearts of his family. Some children have even taken matters into their hands and attempted revenge because of what they heard. In some cases, Pastors' children when grown, resent the church and want nothing to do with her, because of accounts they have heard from their parents.

It is recommended to shield your children from the politics and issues in the church until they are mature enough to understand without resenting God or the church. You cannot de-market your faith and expect them to still follow you. Even when you start sharing information, this should be done constructively with plans of finding solutions and making things better.

Chapter 10

The Cloak of Christianity

If there was anything like being a Christian from the womb, the Minister's child would be the first to qualify. After all, they are from what one would call "holy loins", some can trace at least two generations of Ministers in their lineage. Right from the moment they are born, Christianity is all they know. They are carried to church as infants; as toddlers, they are groomed to recite scriptures, say prayers, and read the Bible. Very early they learn the lingo of the faith - 'Amen', 'Hallelujah', 'Glory to God', 'Hosanna'! and easily fall into the routine of daily devotions, church programs, prayers, and fasting. Even their very first circle of friends is from the church.

Do not get me wrong, these are all good and encouraged. However, there is a danger of assuming your children know the Lord just because they are so immersed in the Christian routine.

Your children wear the cloak of Christianity because you gave it to them, not necessarily because they made the choice themselves. They can then master the art of pretense while committing all sorts of atrocities, right under your nose, for example, visits to a boyfriend can be presented as a church activity and innocently you give permission to go out.

You might respond, "Should I not trust my child?" You should, but you need to remember that your sweet child was born a depraved sinner!

How then do you help your children stop living a life of pretense?

Personal Relationship with God

Everyone must know the Lord personally. It is possible to be a "Christian" and not know God. The children of Israel who were God's covenant children, saw God move in mysterious ways, yet most of them did not know Him (Romans 9:6). **Until your children have a personal encounter with God, they will remain the way they are, even if they live right inside the church.**

Consider Aaron. Aaron worked for God, he was the point man for Moses; his rod had been used for miracles; he saw the power of God, **yet** in the absence of Moses he denied God.

As I pondered on this event in Exodus 32, I became alarmed at the haste with which Aaron built this golden calf, just as God said, *"They have turned aside* **quickly***..."* (Exodus 32:8). It seems he did not even think over it, he did not think about the God he had been following and by whose power he had worked miracles all this while. I asked myself, why did he not say, "Peradventure Moses is dead; the God who brought us out of Egypt is not dead, let me seek His face?"

Then I realized this is the case with Ministers' children. The moment we are away from our parents and the Christian community, we forget the God of our fathers and the foundations of Christianity with which we were brought up.

I was told of a lady who stood up in a bus to preach, giving a recap of one of her Pastor's sermons. While preaching, she got pelted with questions. At a point, she exclaimed, "That is what my daddy (Pastor) said, and it is final." One might pass it off as loyalty but there is a deeper problem: she only knew what her Minister said, she did not know for herself what God had said and why.

Like Moses to Aaron (Exodus 4:14 – 16), parents tend to serve as middlemen between their children and God. They come to church, pray, and generally live moral lives because their parents say they should.   Even if you train your children in the way they should go, to get to the point of not departing from it, each of them must get to know this God for themselves.

This was the case with Elisha. He was a servant of Elijah, but we heard very little about him until he encountered the God of Elijah personally. When Elijah was leaving, he requested only one thing, the anointing, which represents a special relationship with God. No wonder he cried "Where is the God of my father?" That is to say, I want to know you for myself, be with me as you were with my father. I pray that your children cross the bridge (parents) that links them with God and be on the same side with God, where they commune with Him one on one.

May every Minister's child pray just like Elisha, "Where is the God of my parents? I want to know You. I have heard how my parents laid hands on the sick and they recovered, they spoke a word and it came to pass but what about me?" May they yearn like David and say, *As the deer longs for streams of water, so **I** long for you, O God."* (Psalms 42:1 New Living Translation) and as Moses, may we cry out to God *"...I beseech thee, show **ME** thy glory"* (Exodus 33:18)

What can you do as parents? You can lay that foundation. Just as you preach and talk to others to be born again, do the same to your family. Do not assume they are born again. Spend time with them to know if they have made the decision. Pray for them, make it your priority to not rest until they have experienced salvation.

It is a Choice

Teach your children to know that everyone has a choice to make, irrespective of the circumstances surrounding them. Teach them that we are running a personal race and the actions or inactions of our parents will not be a good enough excuse when we stand before God – we will be responsible for our actions.

Below is an excerpt on a sermon my father Apostle Geoffrey D. Numbere, gave to the House of Levi in 2013 titled "Choices".

> We make choices every day. For example, this morning before you came, or any day you are alive, you can decide to eat either bread in the morning or yam in the morning; that is your choice. You may decide to take tea instead of rice, that is your choice. As you go out, you have several dresses; you may decide to pick one; that is your choice.
>
> We make choices every day but there is one area we do not make a choice – who is going to be your mum or your dad. You do not get to choose your parents. Somebody

made the choice on your behalf. Therefore, no matter if your parents are good or bad, your first allegiance is to God who made the choice. So, I may decide to follow God who chose my family for me, or I may decide to go contrary.

Examples of people who made choices.

1. **King Hezekiah**

   Now it came to pass in the third year of Hoshea son of Elah king of Israel, that Hezekiah the son of Ahaz king of Judah began to reign. Twenty and five years old was he when he began to reign; and he reigned twenty and nine years in Jerusalem. His mother's name also was Abi, the daughter of Zachariah. ***And he did that which was right in the sight of the Lord,*** *according to all that David his father did. (2 Kings 18:1-3)*

2. **King Manasseh**

   Manasseh was twelve years old when he began to reign, and reigned fifty and five years in Jerusalem. And his mother's name was Hephzi-bah. ***And he did that which was evil in the sight of the Lord,*** *after the abominations of the heathen, whom the Lord cast out before the children of Israel. 2 Kings 21:1-2*

3. **King Josiah**

   Josiah was eight years old when he began to reign,

and he reigned thirty and one years in Jerusalem. And his mother's name was Jedidah, the daughter of Adaiah of Boscath. ***And he did that which was right in the sight of the Lord,*** *and walked in all the way of David his father, and turned not aside to the right hand or to the left. 2 Kings 22:1-2*

These are three kings who reigned in Judah – Hezekiah who was twenty-five years when he began to reign, was a good king; succeeded by Manasseh who was twelve years when he began to reign but was a bad king.

The one before him was a good king but he came to a privileged situation and he chose to be a bad king. It is a choice he made. The one before him – Hezekiah, chose God. The same throne, the same opportunity, the same privilege, and one made a choice to be godly, the other made a choice to be ungodly.

After Manasseh was Josiah who started his reign at a much younger age – eight years. He was a good king. The one before him was bad but he refused to follow the ways of Manasseh rather, he chose to be good. So, it is a choice, and you do not blame anyone or your parents if you choose to be bad.

Despite the wickedness of his father, in a bad environment, Josiah was good. You can be a good man in a bad place or a good girl in a bad place and it does not matter your age. These were kings who reigned at different ages and at different times on the same throne, but made different choices – to be good or to be bad. If you read the story of their lives, you would see that those who chose to be good ended up well while the ones who chose to be bad ended up badly.

The choice is yours!

Chapter 11

"Hello Dad, I am Pregnant!"

A lot of teens and youth, including Ministers' children, are caught in the web of pre-marital sex. In some cases, it leads to pregnancy. For every parent, this is unimaginably heartbreaking, even more so for a Minister.

For someone who spends a lot of time speaking and advising others about the ills of pre-marital sex, to think that his daughter has made the same mistake despite his advice is heart-wrenching. Those who perceive him as their "enemy" have a field day mocking and taunting him about his failure to enforce in his home, the standards he has been so vocal about all this while. Sometimes he is so embarrassed, he takes a break from ministering.

Unfortunately, he then takes out this pain on his pregnant daughter. Many times, she is sent out of the home; sometimes disowned and completely cut off from the family. Desperate efforts by emissaries to plead for mercy all fall on deaf ears. The teen is left to fend for herself, or if she is lucky, someone takes her in until the child is born. The estrangement can last for many years, well into adulthood. As for the baby, he or she might never see the grandparents for a long time. In some cases, the mother tries to help her child behind her husband's back. Ironically, a son is almost never disowned for getting a girl pregnant. However, the deed is done, an innocent child will be born.

I fully acknowledge that any parent found in such a situation is heartbroken and I do not in any way minimize your pain. However, the truth must be said: no parent should banish his/her daughter because she is pregnant, more so, a Christian and even more serious, a Minister.

The sin committed is fornication, and the guilty ones, are the parents (the teens); the child is innocent. Two lives should not be destroyed because one sin was committed. God expects us to forgive, just as He did forgive us. Remember, no sin is beyond the redemption of God, yet, by your actions, you conclude that the sin of premarital sex is unforgivable when pregnancy is involved. Your focus should be on how to rehabilitate the teen and her unborn child so she can move on with her life, become responsible, and achieve her dreams and aspirations despite the setback of teen pregnancy. Globally, there are organizations: government-owned and non-governmental organizations that preach this message, the church should do more given we are there to save souls.

Perhaps, you find yourself in such a dilemma and have already sent your pregnant daughter out of your home, never to see your face again; God wants you to forgive and bring your child back home. David found himself in a precarious situation with his son Absalom. Absalom had brought great shame and pain to him as well.

After Absalom had killed Amnon for raping his sister, Tamar, he fled and was in exile for 3 years (2 Samuel 13:38,39). However, we see that David's heart longed for Absalom. Despite his crimes, the love of his father did not wane.

However, like most Ministers, David's pride did not allow him to send for his son, even though it was clear he was in great turmoil and wanted to see his son again and bring him back into the family. Joab had to arrange for a wise woman to give a parable.

And, behold, the whole family is risen against thine

handmaid, and they said, Deliver him that smote his brother, that we may kill him, for the life of his brother whom he slew; and we will destroy the heir also: and so they shall quench my coal which is left, and shall not leave to my husband neither name nor remainder upon the earth. (2 Samuel 14:7)

She told the story of how as a widow, she had only two (2) sons. While they played, one brother slew the other. The family, in trying to administer justice, wanted the only surviving son to be killed since he had committed a crime (murder). The crime committed was first against her, but she wanted her only son spared because there was a greater consequence if the judgment was applied- she would be left alone, the family's legacy gone forever.

In summary, she was driving home the point that the events cannot be reversed, hence everyone must move on, and focus on the much bigger problem - saving the child who is alive, their lineage, and legacy.

She also made a very powerful reference – God Himself! He does not respect persons, but even with judgment, He makes a provision for rescue.

All of us must die eventually. Our lives are like water spilled out on the ground, which cannot be gathered up again. ***But God does not just sweep life away; instead, he devises ways to bring us back when we have been separated from him.*** (2 Samuel 14:14 – New Living Translation)

God is merciful, gracious, longsuffering, abundant in goodness and truth (Exodus 34:6). The Bible says, while we were yet sinners, Christ died for us! We see in the judgment of Adam and Eve, He already had plans for redemption (Genesis 3). Amid judgment, mercy was present. Glory to God!

David listened and sent for Absalom even though with a caveat: he was not going to see him. The events that played out after this saw David running away from Absalom, who had almost taken over his kingdom. Who knows if he had completed the reconciliation process, maybe the story might have been different!

Your case might not be pregnancy but maybe drugs or stealing or one extreme vice that has brought disgrace to you.

Permit me to borrow the words of that wise woman - **"fetch home, your banished"** (2 Samuel 14:13). Do not just stop halfway, forgive completely, and address the issues. Let the forgiveness and reconciliation be total and complete.

Maybe, your child is back home, but your forgiveness is not yet complete. You still cannot relate with your daughter as before as the sight of her child or the memory of what your son has done hurts you afresh. God expects our forgiveness to be total and complete. Consider the prodigal son and his father. We see a delinquent son, who wished his father dead, as inheritance is only given at the demise of someone. His father obliged him, but this was only the beginning. He did not even want to be under the guardianship of his father but took off to a far country. After suffering for a while, he came to his senses and decided to go back home and ask to be a servant.

Doesn't this sound familiar? Recovering from a mistake is very difficult. You might be forgiven but things are usually never the same again. You are looked at differently, sometimes, reminded at every opportunity of your "screw-up".

However, the father of the prodigal son showed us things can be different. His forgiveness was total and complete.

> *And he arose, and came to his father. But when he was*
> *yet a great way off, his father saw him, and had*

compassion, and ran, and fell on his neck, and kissed him. And the son said unto him, Father, I have sinned against heaven, and in thy sight, and am no more worthy to be called thy son. But the father said to his servants, Bring forth the best robe, and put it on him; and put a ring on his hand, and shoes on his feet: And bring hither the fatted calf, and kill it; and let us eat, and be merry: For this my son was dead, and is alive again; he was lost, and is found. And they began to be merry.
(Luke 15:20 – 24)

First, he had compassion on his son. Secondly, he demonstrated his love for him – he hugged, kissed him and celebrated him. Thirdly, he restored him to his former place.

Once again, the focus was on the restoration of the lost soul. *"…for this thy brother was dead, and is alive again; and was lost, and is found."* (Luke 15:32)

There is nothing that evokes repentance as much as when mercy is released in place of judgment that is deserved and expected.

I acknowledge the pain such events can cause. However, I ask once again, that you forgive and be reconciled with your daughter or son.

In "I forgive, for my sake" Apostle Geoffrey D. Numbere explains why we should forgive irrespective of the offense.

"UNFORGIVENESS" is a cankerworm that has eaten deep into the lives of individuals, in homes, in society as well as in the church. "UNFORGIVENESS" is a bait which Satan uses to trap people especially Christians. The person who does not forgive finds himself or herself caught in a vicious web of anger, pain, bitterness, suspicion, terrible physical and spiritual afflictions that may even lead to death, now and in eternity. There is no way of quantifying the damages "UNFORGIVENESS" does to a man.

"I FORGIVE, FOR MY SAKE" is another way of highlighting the Lord's Prayer as taught in Matthew 6:12, "FORGIVE US OUR DEBTS, AS WE FORGIVE OUR DEBTOR.

HEART FORGIVENESS AND RELATIONSHIP
"Forgiveness" must be from the heart. It must be complete and total. We must forgive and restore the

relationship; for if we say we have forgiven and do not relate or restore the strained relationship, we have not fully, truly forgiven. Such forgiveness or forgiving is "HALF-FORGIVENESS" OR "HALF-FORGIVING". "Half- forgiveness" was what David gave to Shimei. (2 Samuel 16:5 – 16; 19:15 - 23)

David could be excused for doing so because that was during the dispensation of Law when if God were to introduce the whole truth as it should be (Matthew 19:8) men could not bear it (John 16:12). But not any longer in this dispensation of Grace.

Chapter 12

Dealing with the Prodigal

part from pregnancy, there are other issues that Pastor's children can get entangled with such as drugs, stealing, cultism, and even be rapists. These are extreme cases but are common in Christian homes and especially in the Pastor's home. It is indeed a difficult experience for any parent, talk more of a Pastor. While we do pray they do not happen to us and our children, they can happen.

So how do you handle a prodigal?

Where did the axe head fall?

It is said that broken people, break other people. A child does not suddenly become addicted to pornography, something happened along the line. A child does not suddenly become wayward, something happened somewhere. If you dig further you will find the root of the problem. Do not get carried away by your pain or anger; do not focus on just the act, remember, the aim is to rescue that child.

I remember an incident growing up. We had a young teenager, a Pastor's child whose job was to go around sleeping with the girls in church. He was a teenager but already a Casanova and many young girls fell prey. Well, at some point we decided it was enough and reported him to our teachers. They had several meetings to find out the extent of the damage. Finally, they were ready with their decision and we were all gathered. I remember thinking, he was going to be disciplined severely but something happened. They asked this young boy to explain himself. While talking, he suddenly started crying. We were shocked, that was not our expectation. He then went on to tell how when he started Junior Secondary School, a much older female student took him under her wings and started molesting him. She made him have sex with her regularly, robbing him of his innocence. There was silence. Our hearts broke. He was a victim himself and had only passed on to others his pain. That was the end of the meeting. They took him aside for further counselling.

This is just one example of many. Finding a solution will start from discovering the root of the problem.

Get help!

While it is important to pray, it is not all you need to do. Get help for your child. I know you are a Pastor, but some people specialize in certain areas, like teen coaches, relationship experts, etc. Even in your church, there could be other Pastors who are better at handling certain issues depending on what the problem is.

Also, since it is your child, your emotions might cloud your judgment. It is not a judgment call on your calling if you refer to another person who can be of help. Of course, you will be carried along in the process.

Be open to other solutions in addition to prayers. For example, if the child has a drug problem, send him/her to a drug rehabilitation center. Yes, there is nothing God cannot do, you can pray and that addiction can go, but it is not always the case. Typically, they need to be weaned off the drug problem. Unfortunately, we tend to cloud our sense of reasoning with over-spirituality. Faith without works is dead, so if medicine can help, then by all means use the available options.

Let them experience the consequences

In some cases, you might need to allow them to face the consequences of their action. For example, your child steals an item and brings it home. You discover it and after scolding the child, you devise smart ways to return the item to the owner discreetly. What you have shown your child is that "Daddy is there to cover up for me". It will graduate to bigger offenses. What should you do? Go with the child, with the item to the owner, and let him or her apologize and return the item. Let him experience the embarrassment of returning the stolen item and being identified as the one who took it. He will learn many lessons.

Or your teenage son is caught sleeping with a girl. Several churches have disciplinary methods for such offenses. Ensure it is applied to your child as well without trying to cover it up to avoid embarrassment as the Pastor. That way, your son will learn amongst other things, that he will not get special treatment because he is "Pastor's son".

Show them love
Be loving to your child even in mistakes. Let that love shine through even in discipline. The prodigal son was sure of his father's love. He knew his father would receive him and not drive him out even if in a reduced capacity.

Chapter 13

The Lion and the Bear

As a Minister, it might be baffling how despite all your efforts, your children still get entangled in one vice or the other. You might find yourself asking, "What did I do wrong?". The truth is that it is not necessarily a result of your actions or inactions. There is "the lion and the bear!"

And David said unto Saul, Thy servant kept his father's sheep, and there came a lion, and a bear, and took a lamb out of the flock: And I went out after him, and smote him, and delivered it out of his mouth: and when he arose against me, I caught him by his beard, and smote him, and slew him. (1 Samuel 17:34 – 35)

David was a good shepherd. He told Saul of how he kept his father's sheep. Even when Samuel came to Jesse's house to anoint the king, David was not at home, he was at his duty post, looking after the sheep and had to be sent for (1 Samuel 16:11). He was diligent at his work.

However, we see him explaining his experience while looking after his father's sheep. He had an encounter with the lion and the bear. Several lessons can be learned from his experience.

Lions and bears are predators and eat other animals such as sheep. In this case, they not only targeted David's sheep, but they actually succeeded in taking the sheep on both occasions. The Bible tells us the devil is *like a roaring lion, seeking whom he may devour* (1 Peter 5:8). We already know we have an enemy who is out to attack the Minister's home. You and your home are targets. Do not forget this! Yes, sometimes the enemy succeeds in taking one or more of your children. He might succeed in polluting them despite all your efforts in bringing them upright.

A lot of times, there is that huge disappointment and sense of failure when your child tells you, "I have a boyfriend/girlfriend", "I have been overtaken in pornography", "I have been on drugs" etc. For emphasis, I reiterate that how you handle a child who opens up to you about their struggles or vices, is critical. Overreaction and high-handedness can result in that child never trusting you again. They will never open up to you again to avoid such a scenario. Sometimes, they do not even confess their mistakes, rather it is uncovered, resulting in embarrassment to you and your family. You wonder, "What did I do wrong?", "How could this have happened, despite all my efforts?"

The answer is there is an enemy out there, and sometimes, he can get hold of one of your children even though you might have done all you can and done it right!

In the mouth of that lion, the sheep was helpless and powerless. One would think that there was no hope anymore, that sheep was gone. Sounds familiar? Sometimes, the Minister's child can be so far gone that hope can be lost. One would think there is no coming back.

David did something interesting, he went after the lion (1 Samuel 17:35). It did not matter if the sheep was in the mouth of the lion already; it might even have been half dead; he went after the lion on a rescue mission. That is what you must do as a Minister, go after the enemy, to free your child from the jaws of the devil. Just like the parable of the lost sheep, the Shepherd went after that one sheep that was lost. There is no depth a person can sink to, that the mercy of God cannot reach. There is no sin too dark that the blood of Jesus cannot cleanse.

How do you go after the child? By prayers. We are encouraged that *"…the weapon of our warfare are not carnal but mighty through God to the pulling down of strongholds.."* (2 Corinthians 10:4).

A lot of times we give up on the prodigal. God asks a question, *"Shall the prey be taken from the mighty, or the lawful captive delivered? But thus saith the Lord, Even the captives of the mighty shall be taken away, and the prey of the terrible shall be delivered: for I will contend with him that contendeth with thee, and I will save thy children."* (Isaiah 49:24 – 25)

Yes, the prey can be rescued! Brace up, wipe off that disappointment and go after your child on your knees. The enemy here is the devil.

We are not told if the sheep cried for help or put up a struggle. That was irrelevant. David had one duty and that was to ensure all his sheep were safe irrespective of themselves. It's time to go after your child that the enemy has in his grip and God will give you victory.

David won the contest; he took the sheep out of the mouth of the lion. Now, the lion went after David himself, but again, he fought and killed off the lion (1 Samuel 17:35). With God on your side, victory is sure and you can win every battle against your children and your family.

The other lesson we learn here is that two enemies attacked David – the lion, and the bear. Two different predators, at different times. The enemy never gives up and will come back in different forms to attack your home and your children. It can be exasperating when you have to deal with one vice after the other, sometimes with the same child or more than one of your children. Know that the devil is never tired and will keep trying. You must be on alert, identify him, and never get tired of fighting (praying) for your children. God will surely give victory.

Philippians 4:6 (AMP) tells us to *"…not be anxious or worried about anything, but in everything [every circumstance and situation] by prayer and petition with thanksgiving, continue to make your [specific] requests known to God."* Pray for your children. Pray daily for your children. Just as you pray for your congregation, your children need even more prayers. They are targets of the enemy, there is pressure to meet up with the expectations of people, etc. You need God to bring up your children in the right way. He is there when you are not and can keep and preserve them. Deliberately pray for your children and where they are lost to sin, do not give up on them, but pray until they are rescued and standing in the faith again.

Chapter 14

Your Home, Your First Parish

When it's all said and done, your family is your biggest achievement, your crown, and your jewel. Pastor James Pierce (we fondly call, Pepe), a bosom friend of my father, on one of his visits, asked me and my siblings to stand out with my parents. He told them to look at us, and said, "They are your greatest achievement. If you fail with them, you have failed in your ministry."

Those words have never left me. How would you feel if after leading others to the Lord your family is lost? People will come and go, you will make friends and lose some along the way, but your family will always remain. If you lose them, you have lost everything.

A sermon my mother, Pastor Dr. Nonyem Numbere gave to a gathering of Ministers captures the message aptly. Excerpts below:

> "The Minister's family is always on the front burner for satanic attacks. This is because a Minster whose family is a failure will also be a failure in his ministry, a fact that many Ministers are either ignorant of or decide to ignore.
>
> Many Ministers have become so preoccupied with the church they are overseeing, so busy attending to others that they have neglected their wives and children. From the above, you can see that the saying "Your home is your first parish" applies much more to the Minister than to others. The relationship of God and the believers is the family concept – He is our Father and we are His children and the relationship of Christ with the Church is that of husband and wife:
>
> *For the husband is the head of the wife, even as Christ is the head of the church: and he is the saviour of the body… Husbands, love your wives, even as Christ also loved the church, and gave himself for it;… So ought men to love their wives as their own bodies. He that loveth his wife loveth himself. For no man ever yet hated his own flesh; but nourisheth and cherisheth it, even as the Lord the church:(Ephesians 5:23-29)*

Similarly, God in His relationship with Israel saw Himself as both their husband and their Father (Isaiah 54:5; Jeremiah 3:14; Hosea 2:19). A man who is not a good husband and father is incapable of being a good leader in the house of God.

Abraham was a man of God and he received a commendation from God for the way he managed his household. He led them in the way of God. He was to reap blessings for this including being God's confidant.

And the Lord said, Shall I hide from Abraham that thing which I do; Seeing that Abraham shall surely become a great and mighty nation, and all the nations of the earth shall be blessed in him? For I know him, that he will command his children and his household after him, and they shall keep the way of the Lord, to do justice and judgment; that the Lord may bring upon Abraham that which he hath spoken of him. (Genesis 18:17 – 19)

The leadership of the Home

The Minister is the head of the home in both secular and spiritual matters and he should not be careless about this responsibility.

- **The Priest of the Home**

"Your home is your first parish" and so you need to perform the duties of the priest at home. Set up a family altar assisted by your wife with your children participating in the Bible reading, discussion, and prayers. "The family that prays together sticks together," the saying goes.

In the Old Testament times, the priest's duty in the holy place in the tabernacle was,

i.   To light the lamp, trim it, morning and evening, and cause it to burn always.

ii.   Each time he tended the lamp, he was also to burn incense on the altar of incense which was before the veil (Exodus 27:20-21; 30:8).

iii.   The lamp gave light to the tabernacle and represented Christ, the light of God, and the word of God. The altar of incense was for burning incense which was a symbol of prayers. Therefore, the Minister must have the light of God (Jesus Christ) through His Word and be a person of prayer personally and as a family.

David's last words (2 Samuel 23) were a statement about family.

And he shall be as the light of the morning, when the sun

riseth, even a morning without clouds; as the tender grass springing out of the earth by clear shining after rain. ***Although my house be not so with God;*** *yet he hath made with me an everlasting covenant, ordered in all things, and sure: for this is all my salvation, and all my desire, although he make it not to grow.* (2 Samuel 23: 4, 5)

David was a man after God's heart, a prophet yet he had a failed family – his daughter Tamar was raped by her stepbrother Amnon, who was then killed by Tamar's brother Absalom. Absalom also rebelled against David and raped his concubines. Finally, Adonijah, another of his sons, tried to install himself as king without his father's consent. It is said of him that he grew up doing whatever he wanted to do. His father never asked him where he went to or what he did. (1 Kings 1: 1 – 6)

Do not be a failure in ministry because of a failed family. You can have a good family testimony if you ask God for help."

Show your children the ropes
Involve your family in some of your ministerial duties. Take them along when you go out for evangelism, your preaching engagements, or while visiting the sick. Most importantly,

model Christian virtues for them - let them learn from you how to treat people and live a godly life.

Fan their talents

Every child has a talent or more. This goes beyond musical ability – some children have leadership, administrative traits, etc. Whatever it is, identify the talent and encourage it. The best way to do this is to provide as many opportunities as possible, you may even have cause to call on their talents someday.

As a growing child, I was always hanging around my father's office (which was at the same location as the house) during holidays. I would stay with his staff, mesmerized by the computer which looked like a television box. As I grew older, I would do mundane tasks like sweeping and cleaning. He never drove me away, saying "This place is for adults". I picked up skills, not just using the computer but administrative skills. Well, there was a time, he had no staff. His office was empty. Guess who stood in? That little child who had been hanging around. As I grew older, I became his secretary irrespective of his official staff. I would type his speeches and at a point, I asked him for permission to transcribe his messages to get him started once again on writing his books. He accepted and to the glory of God, his and my mum's books remain my burden till today.

As for musical talents, the fact that the entire family is made up of musicians should not surprise anyone. My mum ensured we got music lessons, bought musical cassettes (I cannot tell you how many of her radio cassette players we destroyed), and even encouraged us to express it. She would take us wherever she was invited to preach for us to sing before she started. She encouraged me to start up a choir in the children's church and quitting was never an option. One time during rehearsals under the mango tree, I got so frustrated, threw the chalk away in anger, and walked out on the choir. My mum was sitting in front of our house watching the scene. As I walked away, I met her gaze. Without a word, she raised her hand towards me which meant "go back". I stopped in my tracks, threw a little tantrum, and went right back to continue teaching. That mantle of leadership was passed on to the next sibling in order of seniority as each of us graduated from the children's department. Not because we were the children of the leader, but because our gifts of leadership and music had been nurtured and grown.

Your target should be to raise your children to the point they can bear your burdens (both spiritually and physically) with you just as Aaron and Hur helped Moses.

> *But Moses hands were heavy; and they took a stone, and*
> *put it under him, and he sat thereon; and Aaron and Hur*
> *stayed up his hands, the one on the one side, and the other*

on the other side; and his hands were steady until the going down of the sun. (Exodus 17:12)

Model Christian virtues

Abraham lived with his nephew Lot until they had to split when their households grew too big. In Genesis 18, we see Abraham being hospitable to strangers he sighted under the hot sun. In the very next chapter (Genesis 19), we see Lot, his nephew, do exactly the same thing; he invited the guests into his house and insisted that they accept his invitation.

I do not know where they picked this trait but even when they were apart, Lot continued to exhibit the hospitable qualities his uncle had.

Another example is my dear mother, Pastor Nonyem E. Numbere. She showed us practically how to treat everyone equally. How? She cared for her large family equally. Growing up, we had at least 20 to 25 people at any given time under her roof. If she could not give items such as clothes to everyone, no one got, even me, her only daughter. Also, in discipline, the same rules applied to everyone. Live-in housekeepers were treated the same. It was standard practice to train everyone either in school or in a trade based on your choice or ability, so it was a common feature to find the faithful housekeepers, leave the house with educational degrees, or at marriage.

These principles have been fully imbibed in us all and we relate in the same way till today. When I talk about my family, I am referring to at least 25 other people other than my siblings. We love ourselves dearly and treat each other like we were born from the same womb.

My parents also got us into studying our Bibles by not just having morning devotions but also showed us the ropes practically. We studied the Bible sequentially from Genesis to Revelation, chapter by chapter, and had to lead morning devotion in turns according to seniority. Basically, you would be the Pastor for the day. You would be responsible for gathering everyone at 5 am for devotion, lead praise and worship, organize the Bible reading, then explain the lessons derived from the study. Of course, my parents would critique your sermon on the spot. Even if you were part of the congregation that day, you did not get away easily - there was time for "contribution" where at least three people would also explain what they had learned. When this was over, either of my parents would then explain the same lesson to us. When it was time for prayer, the Pastor for the day would also lead the session. We did this every day without fail and this practice is still on!

By the way, if you did not deliver the sermon properly, you had to repeat your turn. I remember our youngest cousin at that time. No matter what the Bible study was, his contribution would be, "I learnt that we should love one another". As the youngest toddler, my dad would exclaim, "Good boy, everybody clap for him". We would all give him a round of applause. Well, he grew and outgrew his favorite line. One of those days he said, "I learnt that we should love one another", my mum did not accept it, not anymore. She insisted he must give a proper lesson relevant to the Bible reading. He learnt his lesson that day and had to start studying his Bible properly.

What did this do for us? We learned to study the Bible, how to pray, public speaking, and taking responsibility amongst others. Of course, initially, we did not find this palatable neither were we experts at this. Someone once prayed "Lord, we pray for the Governor, that you will give him a retentive memory". We had a good laugh, but we grew, we matured in the things of God. As we grew older, we got to know the Lord personally. Our devotions were special, the presence of God was mighty, insights into the Holy Scriptures were revealed. It is a period in my life I will always cherish.

Point your children to God

God's plan was for the Levites to be totally given to His service. They were not to own lands or property because God was their inheritance. Thus, their daily upkeep was to come from the sacrifices offered at the Temple.

It is the same thing today; the Minister should be sustained by the church. He and his family expect love and physical provisions from the congregation, and rightfully so. Unfortunately, it has led many Ministers to have cliques, show favoritism and even pervert justice in favor of that one person whose tithe is large or those who regularly bring gifts to them.

Sometimes, there is an entitlement mentality, where the Minister and his family earmark certain congregants (by the type of car they drive, clothes they wear, etc.) and make outrageous demands of them. After all, they have so much money, they should include the Minister and his family as their responsibility. Thus, a lot of pressure is put on the congregation. When the demands are not met, it results in great frustration.

We must fix our eyes on God alone. **He and only He is the inheritance of the Minister**. The duty of the people is to serve God with their lives, their substances and ultimately, look after the Minister. God will use people no doubt, but your source and confidence should be on God. David said he had *never seen the righteous forsaken or his seed begging bread* (Psalm 37:25). Never take your eyes off the real source of provision, that is, God.

Teach your children to depend on God and keep their hope

firmly in Him, just as Abraham told Isaac *"God Himself will provide..."* (Genesis 22:8). The scriptures abound with instances of this – Joseph saving his family from famine (Genesis 50:20); ravens feeding Elijah (1 Kings 17:6); the coin found in the fish (Matthew 17:27). I am also sure you have testimonies of God's miraculous provision. There is absolutely nothing God cannot do. Teach your children to fix their eyes only on Him.

Spiritual Experiences

God promised to pour out His Spirit on all flesh (Joel 2:28). Some children begin to experience the supernatural at a very young age. They receive Christ into their lives and become baptized in the Holy Spirit even as children or teens. This is what we pray for, the earlier the better; after all, the devil does not consider age when he wants to use a person. However, we have seen cases where children or teens who manifest the gifts of the Holy Spirit such as speaking in tongues or prophecy, are stopped because it is assumed that they are too young to understand the infilling of the Holy Spirit.

The question is, "Is there a specified age for one to experience God and His Spirit?" The answer is "No". We see where God told Jeremiah not to think that he is too small (Jeremiah 1:7), we read of Paul telling Timothy, let no man despise your youth (1 Timothy 4:12) amongst others.

As a Minister, observe that child and guide him/her aright. Do not discountenance their spiritual experiences or wave them off as childish pranks, rather encourage and provide the necessary guidance to ensure the child grows in God and the devil does not take advantage and another spirit fills the child.

Autocracy versus Democracy

The pressure to ensure the family tows the same line sometimes makes the Minister very autocratic with his family. He also expects his beliefs to be accepted without question. However, this generation does not follow orders without understanding the whole concept – we will always ask "Why?".

You see, as your children grow up, they begin to question the traditions and beliefs you have taught them. It is important to allow them to ask questions and be ready to answer truthfully. Be open to have those difficult conversations. At least, it gives you an idea of the thoughts of your child and you have the opportunity to explain or correct. It also gives you the opportunity to learn something new and I must warn, sometimes you might have to change your stand on certain traditions.

We see in the scripture two examples: The daughters of

Zelophehad in Numbers 26 who questioned the law of only males keeping an inheritance. Moses, listened to them, consulted God and a change was implemented. We also see in Acts 15, the Apostles had to have a difficult conversation on if the Gentiles needed to be circumcised. Remember that circumcision was a sign of the covenant of God with Israel, yet this was deliberated upon by the Church. They made some adjustments – the Gentles will not be forced to be circumcised but told them the practices they must keep (Acts 15:20).

Do not shut down that child that asks questions like an "unbeliever". Take your time to prayerfully expound the scriptures to help him/her understand and not "It is that way, because I said so", or "This is what we believe or nothing else".

My parents did their best to answer our questions. My brother, Kaydee Numbere put it aptly in a tribute to them:

> We always had our morning devotion by 5 am and did not skip ANY part of the scripture. I cannot count the number of times we finished the Bible from Genesis to Revelation. Now, this gave us the opportunity to discuss the complex issues as it was impossible to skip any matter. We would spend time debating with my dad. Sometimes our questions were so HARD he would go back to research so he could answer us the next day whilst not seeing us as his children who knew NOTHING.

I have seen Ministers' children who have become atheists just because their questions were suppressed. It only festered and when they became adults, they did a 180-degree turn. Even if they do not have questions, ensure they understand the principles behind the Christian beliefs so that they would not be swayed when not under your care.

Set standards and boundaries

It is important to set standards and boundaries at home. The fact that you want to appear loving to your children does not mean you should not be a parent or be at their mercy. Are they accountable? Do they have bedtime and lights out? Do they know how to respect their elders? Are you aware of the gifts they receive? There must be standards and principles in your home.

As mentioned earlier, the fact that you bring your children up with the required Christian practices of prayer, reading the word of God and fellowship, does not mean you should throw caution to the wind in raising your children. Do not let your guard down or feel at ease because you are in a Christian community. Right in church, your child can be exposed to vices, predators, and rapists. Do not relax because you believe we are all "brethren". Ensure you have rules and standards at home, you know their friends, and their movements etc. For example, keeping late nights or returning home late at night should not be allowed to happen even if it is for a supposed church program. As mentioned previously, discipline your child appropriately and as required.

If they love you, they should love your family
The Bible encourages every believer to care for the Minister. Generally speaking, a Minister who loves and cares for his congregation, would thus have this love reciprocated. The natural tendency is for people to concentrate or pay attention to the Pastor only – after all, he is directly involved in caring for them. You find members of the congregation caring for the Pastor only, forgetting he has a family. Family boundaries are not respected, and sometimes, outright disrespect is shown to his spouse. My mum described it as "daughters who have daddies but no mummies" and "sons who have mummies but no daddies"!

It must be stated, however, that in a lot of cases, this disrespect thrives because the Pastor does not know where to draw the line in relating with his congregation.

Growing up, my parents were always on the move going about God's work. The constant visits to the house, supply of food, and other items when my parents were around quickly disappeared as soon as they travelled. Only a few people would still check on us to know how we were doing. The return of the visitors always coincided with their return. Then we would answer questions on end from people asking about our welfare.

It gets worse in cases of the demise of the Minister: his family is completely forgotten. Nobody asks how they are coping with the loss and as soon as the mourning period is over, life goes on and everyone moves on. It is only natural that the attention on the late Pastor's family would reduce, but they should not be neglected. Yes, the Minister should plan for his family and train them to be independent, but if the people had also loved his family, that gap would not be so wide.

The Apostle John wrote his second epistle to someone he called "The elect lady"; not just to her, but her children also. He declared his love for her and her children.

> *The elder unto the elect lady and her children, whom I love in the truth; and not I only, but also all they that have known the truth;* (2 John 1:1)

If anyone loves you, they should love your family as well. Encourage members of your congregation to build relationships with your family. Where possible and as necessary, involve your family in these relationships. For example, go along with your spouse or children to pay visits, that way relationships are established with not just you, but your family. The congregation should also be encouraged to extend their benevolence to the entire family. We have seen instances of people bringing one serving of food to the Minister's house, despite the fact he has a family of 5 or even 7. What message is being passed? That portion could have been increased to at least accommodate at the minimum the Minister and his wife.

If they really love you, they would love your family. Make it clear that you are one with your family and all that show of love should be extended to your loved ones.

Chapter 15

God's Intention

The journey of a child from conception to delivery, then to maturity is such a beautiful one that cannot be fully described. No wonder the Psalmist says,

For thou hast possessed my reins: thou hast covered me in my mother's womb. I will praise thee; for I am fearfully and wonderfully made: marvellous are thy works; and that my soul knoweth right well. My substance was not hid from thee, when I was made in secret, and curiously wrought in the lowest parts of the earth. Thine eyes did see my substance, yet being unperfect; and in thy book all my members were written, which in continuance were fashioned, when as yet there was none of them. (Psalm 139:13-16)

A child is indeed a gift from God. Medical science can help and advice, but the actual conception is only by the power of God. Your children are gifts from God. Let nothing make you think otherwise. When we speak of children here, we refer to both biological and adopted.

God's plan for the Minister's child is fully described in Psalm 127:3 -5

> *Lo, children are an heritage of the LORD: and the fruit of the womb is his reward. As arrows are in the hand of a mighty man; so are children of the youth. Happy is the man that hath his quiver full of them: they shall not be ashamed, but they shall speak with the enemies in the gate.*

Arrows In The Hand Of A Mighty Man

The strength of the arrow lies in the ability of the user. On its own, an arrow is useless, in the hands of a child, it could be a toy and even harm him, but in the hands of a mighty man, it becomes a deadly weapon.

This is what sets apart one Minister's child from another. One is in the hand of a "mighty man" (God) and the other is left to the devil. A common factor is that they will be used, whether by God or by the devil. The question is "In whose hands, are your children?"

Isaiah said,

> *Behold, I and the children whom the LORD hath given me are for signs and for wonders in Israel from the LORD of hosts, which dwelleth in mount Zion.* (Isaiah 8:18)

This is where your family should be, full of the anointing and power of God and used by God for signs and wonders.

Also, a bow is required to propel the arrow. That bow represents you, our God-given parents (especially Ministers of the Gospel). Once nocked and released, the arrow moves as directed. As Ministers, you must direct your children aright. Lead them in the way they should go and when they are old, they will not depart from it (Proverbs 22:6).

They Shall Not Be Ashamed

The next thing the Psalmist says is that the children will not be ashamed. They will be confident and proud of their home and their parents. I pondered on this and realized a lot of children are ashamed: ashamed of the fact that they are Pastor's children, ashamed of the Ministry he is called into, ashamed that their parents do not have mansions and exotic cars, ashamed that they are not allowed to be like others. They feel inferior and refuse to identify with their parents or their Ministry. Many children brag about their parents' occupation: "My dad is an engineer, he works in XY Energy Company". However, it is quite rare to find one who would brag about his dad being a Pastor. Things might have changed a bit with time, but typically, this is the case.

Most times, the Minister's children look at men to reward their parents, and when it seems they are not getting what the world uses as a yardstick for success – cars, houses, etc., they look down on their office. But there is more to it. Ministers, as my beloved spouse puts it are "direct employees of God" and we know that the God we serve is not unfaithful; He rewards all that diligently seek Him. He says it clearly in Matthew 7:11,

> *If ye then, being evil, know how to give good gifts unto your children, how much more shall your Father which is in heaven give good things to them that ask him?*

And in Hebrews 11:6b '*…he is a rewarder of them that diligently seek Him'*

It is all about perception. Let us consider what happens around us. Every company/institution is responsible for the welfare of its employees. In like manner, our heavenly Father is able to take care of His own. We are His responsibility as His children, and much more as His Ministers. God is very clear about this; He is the portion of the Levites.

It is again, all about perception. Being blessed is not about the amount of money, houses, or cars you acquire. It transcends physical acquisitions. True blessings include love, warmth, a loving home, a good name, and most importantly, being saved.

By the grace of God, our home was what you can call blessed, not by the standards of the world as we did not have riches in abundance but one thing that was in abundance was lots of love and warmth. As a matter of fact, the more we were, the merrier it was. The moment any person moved out, we would look for more people to move in and sleep on the ground with us. We called ourselves 'The Numbere community' which included four dogs, and now called "The GRA Family". We learnt to love without restrictions, we learnt to share even when it was not comfortable, we learnt to be abased and raised. I say it with pride, we are blessed!

Let us also consider other benefits - the gift of life, protection, sound health, safety, etc. How much do we pay for these? How about favour and a good name? My dad has passed on but now and again, when I meet someone who knew him, I beam with pride as they extol his virtues and talk about him with so much adoration. Of course, they treated me well just because of my dad and the legacy he left.

Dear Minister, teach your children to understand the spiritual inheritance, understand that it is a privilege to be a Minister. God told Moses that in place of lands and houses, He would be the inheritance of the Levites.

Teach them to see who they are in Christ, the privileges they have as children of God, the extra privileges as children of Ministers. Teach them that even though you are just men and women, you are also servants of the Most High God, His mouthpiece in these times, and the God whom you serve, will never leave you stranded.

Do not feel inferior or ashamed but exude the kind of pride in your calling and contentment that is contagious. Let it radiate to your family and everyone around you. Raise your children to be proud to say, "My parents are servants of the Most High God". God, Himself will reward you for your labours.

Speak with the Enemy at the Gate
These children will 'speak with the enemy at the gate'. The man at the gate is the first access anyone must see before he/she gets into the house. It is this man that says, 'You can come in' or 'You cannot'. He takes action, nothing passes without his approval and the Psalmist refers to this gateman as 'children of one's youth' or a man's children.

This is God's intention – that your children should stand at the 'gate' of your homes and families spiritually and determine what happens; that they fight the enemy at the gate, not when he is already in the house causing havoc, no! Rather you can go to sleep knowing they have 'the gate' covered spiritually on their knees.

A typical example was Jonathan, who always went to battle with his father, Saul. In 1 Samuel 13 and 14, we read an interesting story. Jonathan attacked a Philistine garrison. When he does, King Saul boasts about it and the story goes around that it was Saul who had defeated them. Saul got accolades for his son's exploits!

There was more trouble: the Philistines regrouped and returned with a larger army, and the Israelites hid in caves. Even Saul, who was supposed to be a courageous leader, lost heart. When Samuel the prophet, did not arrive in time to offer the pre-battle sacrifice, he offered it himself and incurred God's anger and subsequent rejection.

While everyone was hiding, Jonathan took the initiative to deal with the enemy. In his own words to his armour bearer,

> *Come, and let us go over unto the garrison of these uncircumcised: it may be that the LORD will work for*

us: for there is no restraint to the LORD to save by many or by few. (1 Samuel 14:6)

Jonathan, the child of Saul 'spoke with the enemy at the gate'. He told his armour bearer to go with him to the garrison of the Philistines. It was there he attacked the Philistines, in their camp (the gate) before they could approach the Israelites.

And God stood by him.

And Jonathan climbed up upon his hands and upon his feet, and his armourbearer after him: and they fell before Jonathan; and his armourbearer slew after him...And there was trembling in the host, in the field, and among all the people: the garrison, and the spoilers, they also trembled, and the earth quaked: so it was a very great trembling. (1 Samuel 14:13, 15)

The result was that Israel won the battle, all because of Jonathan. *So the LORD saved Israel that day: and the battle passed over unto Bethaven.* (1 Samuel 14:23)

Oh, that we might have such bold children, who will tread where great men or maybe even their parents fear to tread; children who will take over your battles; children who will stand by you even when you are weak.

It takes a man who is not ashamed to speak and act with boldness – Jonathan properly classified the Philistines the way God saw them – uncircumcised. Remember, the covenant of the Israelites with God was sealed by circumcision. In this statement, Jonathan was declaring he was a child of God, so the people before him were nothing compared to who he was.

It takes a man who is proud of his home to defend it. Dear Minister, you need the help of your family, to uphold you and your ministry in prayers and to assist in your work. No one can stand by you more than your family, who love you more than anyone else.

Pour out His Spirit

God's intention for our families is also to pour out His Spirit on all. We see that in Joel 2:28 when He makes this promise.

> *And it shall come to pass afterward, that I will pour out my Spirit upon all flesh; and your sons and your daughters shall prophesy, your old men shall dream dreams, your young men shall see visions:*(Joel 2:28)

In the Old Testament, we see that the Spirit of God was poured out on a select few. These chosen vessels would then stand out as God's oracle at that point in time. Glory be to God; we see in Joel 2:28 a reversal. God promises to pour out His Spirit on all flesh -

an outburst of God's Spirit. God promises an outpour, a downpour of His Spirit until we are soaked and drenched, pouring and dripping with the Spirit of God! Hallelujah!

This promise was fulfilled in Acts 2 on the day of Pentecost:

> *And when the day of Pentecost was fully come, they were all with one accord in one place. And suddenly there came a sound from heaven as of a rushing mighty wind, and it filled all the house where they were sitting. And there appeared unto them cloven tongues like as of fire, and it sat upon each of them. And they were all filled with the Holy Ghost, and began to speak with other tongues, as the Spirit gave them utterance.* (Acts 2:1 – 4)

Peter stood up and explained to the wondering crowd that the prophecy in Joel had been fulfilled. In his words,

> *For these are not drunken, as ye suppose, seeing it is but the third hour of the day. But this is that which was spoken by the prophet Joel; And it shall come to pass in the last days, saith God, I will pour out of my Spirit upon all flesh: and your sons and your daughters shall prophesy, and your young men shall see visions, and your old men shall dream dreams: And on my servants and on my handmaidens I will pour out in those days of*

my Spirit; and they shall prophesy: **For the promise is unto you, and to your children,** *and to all that are afar off, even as many as the LORD our God shall call.* (Acts 2:15 – 18, 39).

God promised to pour out His Spirit upon all flesh! No discrimination – everyone! And to make sure we fully understand what He means, He gives specifics: **"Your sons and Your daughters".** In this phrase God addresses several things:

- **Age**

There is no age limit to this outpour. Paul told Timothy, *"let no man despise your youth…"* (1 Timothy 4:12).

Do not think your children are too young to be filled with the Spirit of God. As a matter of fact, the devil even fills children much earlier; we hear of child soldiers or those who were initiated into occult groups as little children. All God wants is a willing vessel to fill; age or race does not matter. This should be your prayer for your children.

- **Gender**

God also addresses gender here, by specifically mentioning daughters. The Spirit of God is not just for boys/men but for girls/women. Examples abound in the Bible of women who were chosen by God, Deborah, Mary Magdalene who was the first to see Jesus after resurrection to mention but a few.

- **Households**

We also see God addressing entire households – your sons **and** your daughters. The heartbeat of God is that everyone in an entire house is filled with His Spirit, not just a few of them.

Dear parents, please do not be satisfied that one or two of your children are fervent and serving God; the promise is for every single member of your family – your sons and your daughters. Do not be satisfied that all your children know the Lord except one. This promise is also meant for him/her. Just as the shepherd left the ninety-nine in search of just one lost sheep, do not rest until that child is back into the fold and serving God.

We are in the dispensation of the Holy Spirit (the Spirit of God). Apostle Numbere, my father, commenting on Ephesians 5:18 (*"and be not drunk with wine wherein is excess; but be filled with the Spirit;"*), said, "A drunkard is not aware of his surroundings; alcohol is fully in control. It can move him four steps forward and then turn him around in another direction; it can make a well-dressed man sit in the gutter or stand in the middle of a busy road. A man under the influence of alcohol has no fear; he can do or say anything because he is no longer in control – alcohol has taken the driving seat."

Medically, alcohol is a drug that is absorbed into the bloodstream from the stomach and intestine. Until it is broken down, it continues to circulate the bloodstream, affecting all of the body's organs including the brain.[3]

We are to be filled with the Holy Spirit, completely controlled by Him. He should take over our brain, our heart, our entire being, and control every part of our body, speech, decisions, movement, actions - everything. No wonder a timid Peter was able to stand up and declare God's word on the day of Pentecost, disciples who were in hiding came out speaking boldly. It is interesting to note they were termed as drunkards. That's right, they were completely under the influence of the Holy Spirit.

The Holy Spirit comes with power, Jesus said, "...*You shall receive power after the Holy Spirit is come upon you...*" (Acts 1:8). Jesus knew how vital it is to have the Spirit of God that He told His disciples not to go anywhere but stay in Jerusalem and wait (no evangelism, no follow-up) until they received the outpour. We can do nothing without the Holy Spirit.

It is the Holy Spirit that gives us power, the spirit of boldness, and a sound mind such that we can *subdue kingdoms, wrought righteousness, obtain promises, stop the mouths of lions, quench the violence of fire, wax valiant in fight and turn to flight the armies of the enemies* (Hebrews 11:33,34).

---

[3] http://www.pamf.org/teen/risk/alcohol/effectonbody.html
Palo Alto Medical Foundation

It is the Holy Spirit that can change your child into "another man". Just like Saul became "another man", that is, a different man when He received the Spirit of the Lord. Samuel had anointed him (1 Samuel 10:1) and told him he would prophesy with other prophets after the Spirit of the Lord came on him.

Two phrases stand out: "turned into another man" (1 Samuel 10:6) and "God gave him another heart" (1 Samuel 10:9).

The Spirit of the Lord changes a man completely. He is what your children need.

Chapter 16

Households of Faith

My father (Apostle Numbere) once made a prophetic statement. He said, "This is the season of Households. We are in a time when 'entire Households' will come on board and serve the Lord." Glory to God!

We can see in the Bible, households of faith and households of shame. Some 'households of faith' include

    a.   Abraham, his son Isaac and grandson, Jacob (Israel)

    b.   Aaron the priest, his son Eleazar and his grandson, Phinehas

    c.   Amongst the disciples of Jesus, we have brothers (Luke 6:13 – 16)

        i.   Simon Peter and Andrew his brother

> ii.   James the son of Zebedee and John his brother
>
> iii.   James the son of Alphaeus and Judas his brother (not Iscariot)

d.   Timothy, his mother Eunice, and grandmother Lois

'Households of shame' include:

a.   Eli and his sons – Hophni and Phinehas

b.   Samuel and his sons – Joel and Abiah

In our time, 'Households of shame' seem to be prevalent. We are in a time when 'households' are given to sin and the world; when faithful men breed unfaithful children and 'terrors' to the devil, breeding 'terrors' to the church.

An example is Samuel. Unfortunately, this great servant of God did not have children worthy to fill his shoes. According to the custom, he made his sons Joel and Abiah judges in Beersheba. However, they did not walk in his ways but perverted judgment and took bribes. (1 Samuel 8:1 – 3)

One is tempted to ask, how come such a servant of God, who served the Lord from childhood, who witnessed what happened to Eli and his family, was still unable to bring up godly children?

They were rather a disgrace and caused Israel to ask for a king, ultimately rejecting God.

One lesson we learn here is that it is not by power or by might, it is by the mercy and grace of God that we can have children who will not be a disgrace to us or our lineage. We also learn here that it is very possible to live in God's house and not be God's child. This is what we see today, lots of 'Joels and Abiahs' – children of God's servants, very active in church, 'working for God' yet committing atrocities in God's house, stealing, lying, living in fornication, luring others to sin and the worst of it all is the fact that others would look at them and say 'Haven't you seen Pastor's child? My sin is not half of what he/she is doing'.

Since Samuel's sons did not follow in his footsteps, the children of Israel demanded a king. Amongst other reasons, they did not want to be led by Samuel's sons, for they were not sure what their lives would be like under the leadership and guidance of his sons. Yes, the actions or inactions of our families can cause others to sin against God, just as Joel and Abiah caused the children of Israel to sin by asking God for a king. The actions of your family can have consequences that go beyond your home! Some we might be aware of, others we may never know. May God help us.

In contrast to Samuel and his sons, we see a wonderful example with Philip the evangelist. He was a great servant of God whom God used to the point where his mode of transportation was by the Spirit of God but he did not just stop there, his household was a household of faith, filled with the power and Spirit of God. (Acts 21:8, 9)

All his daughters prophesied, not one or two; all four! It is not surprising that Philip did exploits for God (Acts 8), his home was a household of faith.

May God bring you and your entire family not just into His kingdom but into active service in fulfilment of Psalm 127: 3 – 5. Some people may say (as they have also said of my family), "Are you the only ones in church? Why is everything being done by members of this family?" With joy and gladness, tell them: the promise is for us all; no exemptions!

Boldly say like Joshua:
> ....*but as for me and my house, we will serve the* LORD.
> (Joshua 24:15)

Conclusion

In conclusion, I would like to reiterate that I am by no means an expert, and raising children is not an experiment with a guaranteed outcome. There are instances where everything seems to have been done right, yet the Minister's child still leaves the faith. In the same home, one child might turn out well and the other different. You might ask why? I do not know.

For some, the journey to becoming a mature Christian might be short; for, others it may be long. Some are yet to find their footing in Christ. What I know, however, is that your prayers and the foundation you lay are not in vain. I know my parents prayed fervently for every one of us and we see the results in our lives.

I encourage you to carry out a round-table activity with your children. Take time out to talk frankly with your children. Ask them to tell you how they honestly feel about you. Where you need to make amends, please start by saying "I am sorry!". Where they need to make amends, they should also apologize. Agree on action plans that would help the relationship going forward. At some point in my life, my father did this. He asked my siblings and me, to be honest with him. The discussion was very enlightening to him, as he discovered a lot of his actions that hurt us, which he was oblivious of. He then apologized to us all. Did that mean there were no longer ups and downs? The answer is "No", but things did change for the better.

We have the assurance of God that His grace is sufficient! His grace that gives supernatural ability to do the impossible is available to direct, guide, and help parents, in particular Ministers in the upbringing of their children.

We pray that grace be multiplied to every Minister! We pray that homes be healed! We pray that our families become households of faith! We pray that our children will be arrows in the hands of a Mighty God!

Levites' Song

There's a voice crying out in our time
In a world of sin, deceitfulness and woe
Who's for Me and who will be on My side?
The Lord calls

So, we gird ourselves and rise and take a stand
Yes, we're different, special, set apart for Him
For the Lord is our inheritance and we are His

Offspring of God's priests

We are called by the Most High
Separated, Selected
We are called
We're the Levites
At the Lord's side we'll stand
Called by the Most High
Consecrated, we're holy
We are called
We're the Levites
Unashamed, Chosen ones